The photos of the sun and other similar images herein are presented with a harsh warning for those wishing to do similar things with something as bright as our home star. That warning is - "don't do it." As simple as it may seem, even something as projecting images on a much larger screen as in using a cellphone can pose damaging-to-the-eyes harm to your vision.  One might ask, 'why then did I do it?' The answer is simple – I needed to and aimed my camera in the general direction of the subject and let fly while not looking. I never even glanced at the screen on the back of my camera until I've made sure I pulled it away from the subject and then examined the results while in a nearby shadow.

# *Sun*

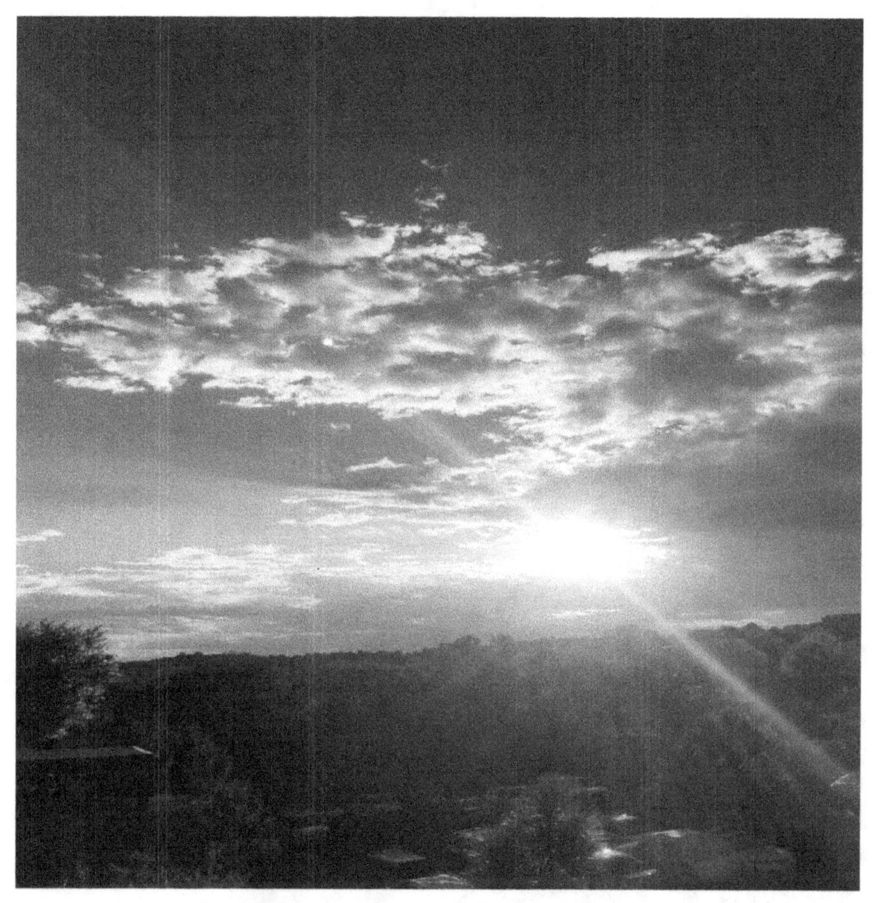

# Photographs
# By
# David Cope

Sun

Photographs by David Cope

This book is dedicated to my wife, sons, and grandchildren, Zoe, Tess, Gavin, and Ethan whose excitement for everyday things never ceases to amaze me. And to those older kids like me who believe in those children.

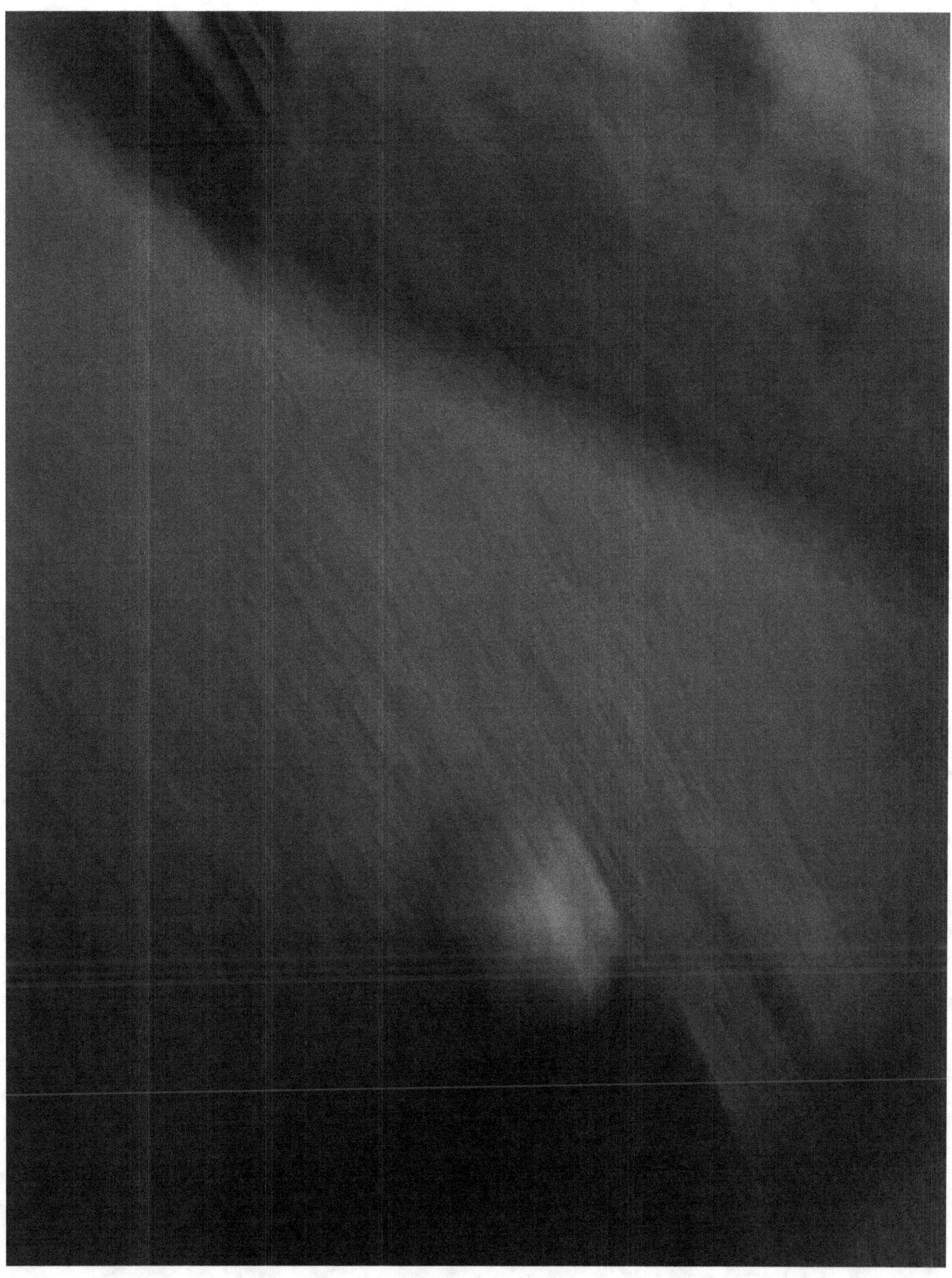

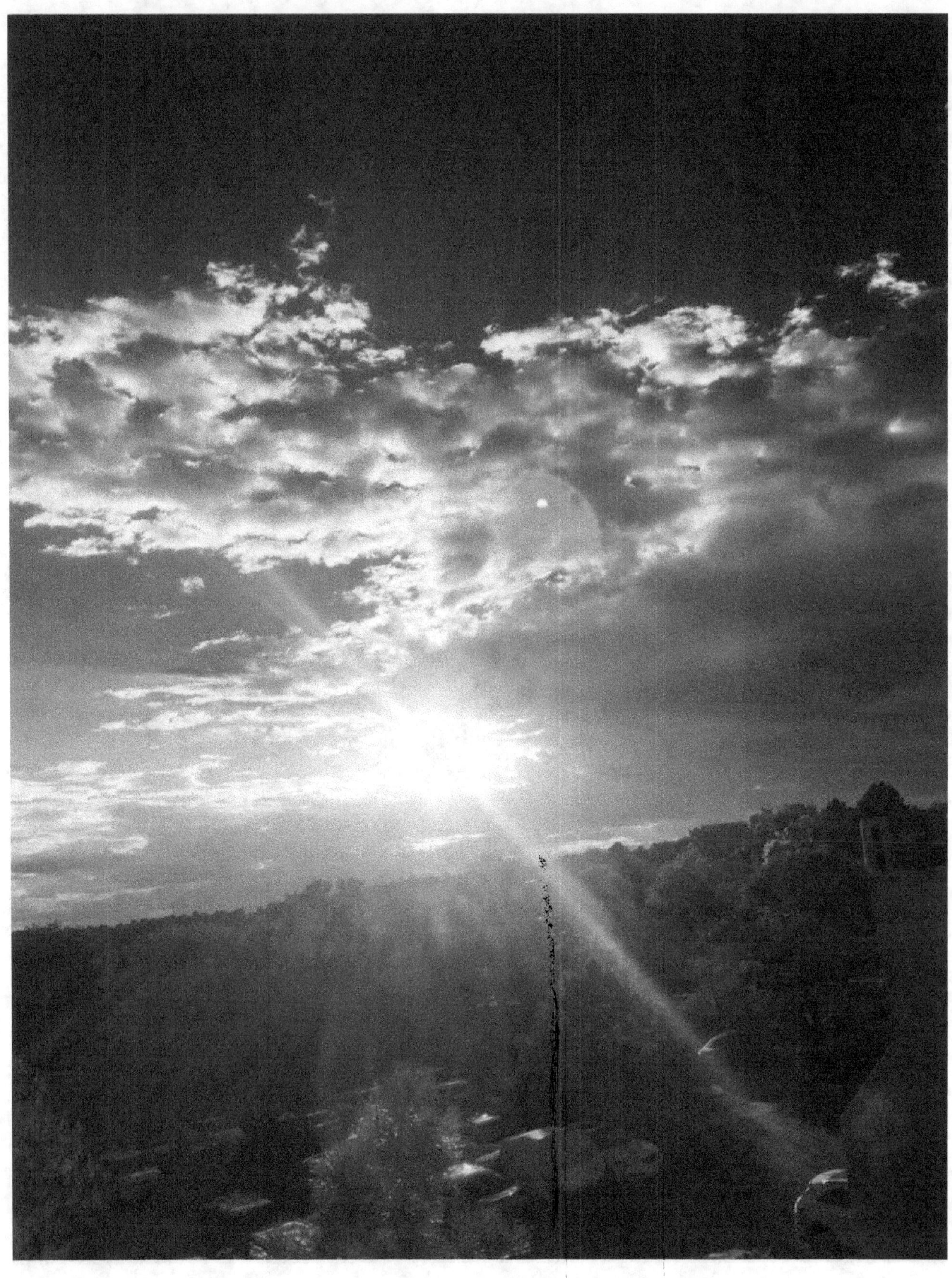

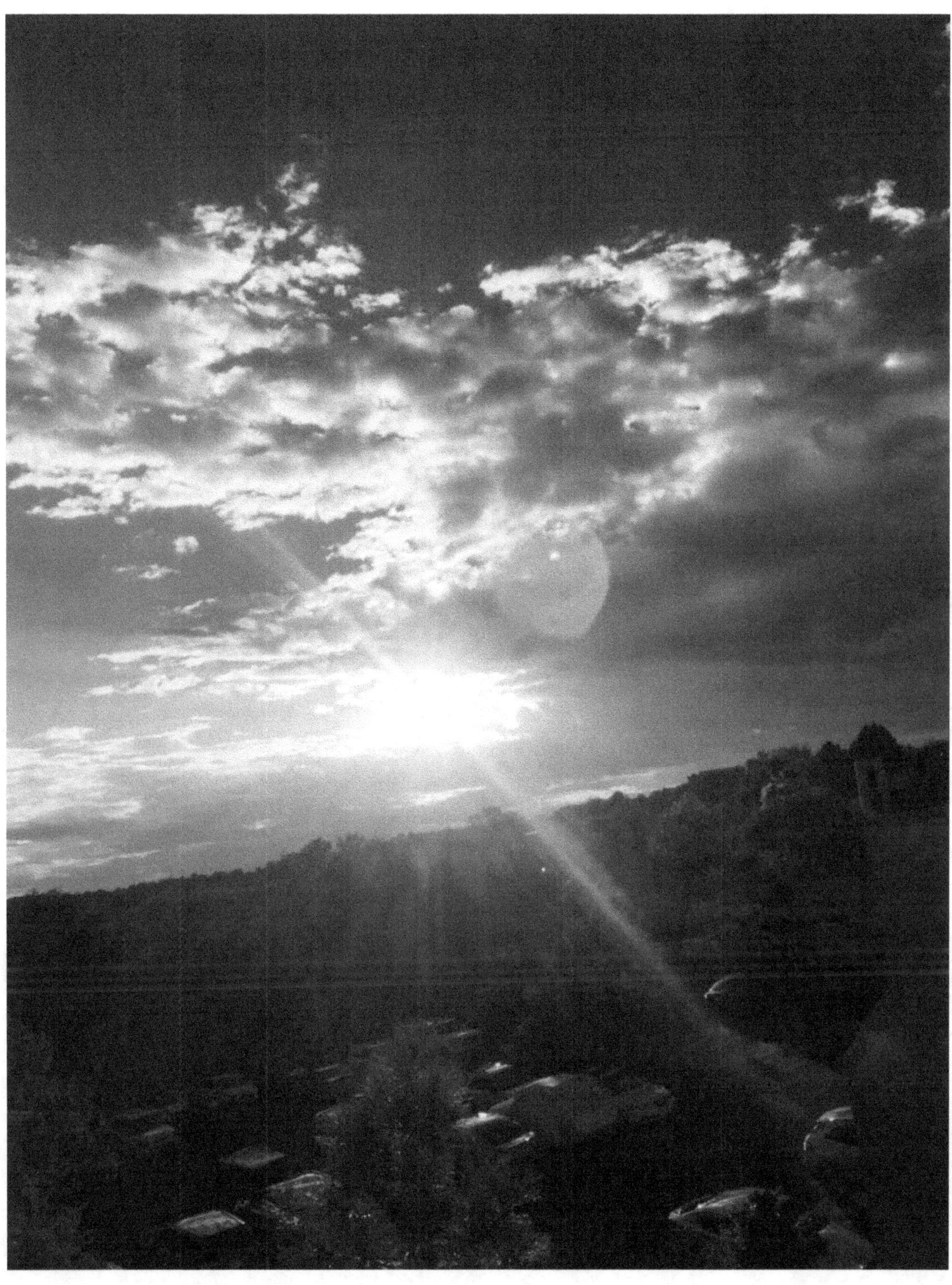

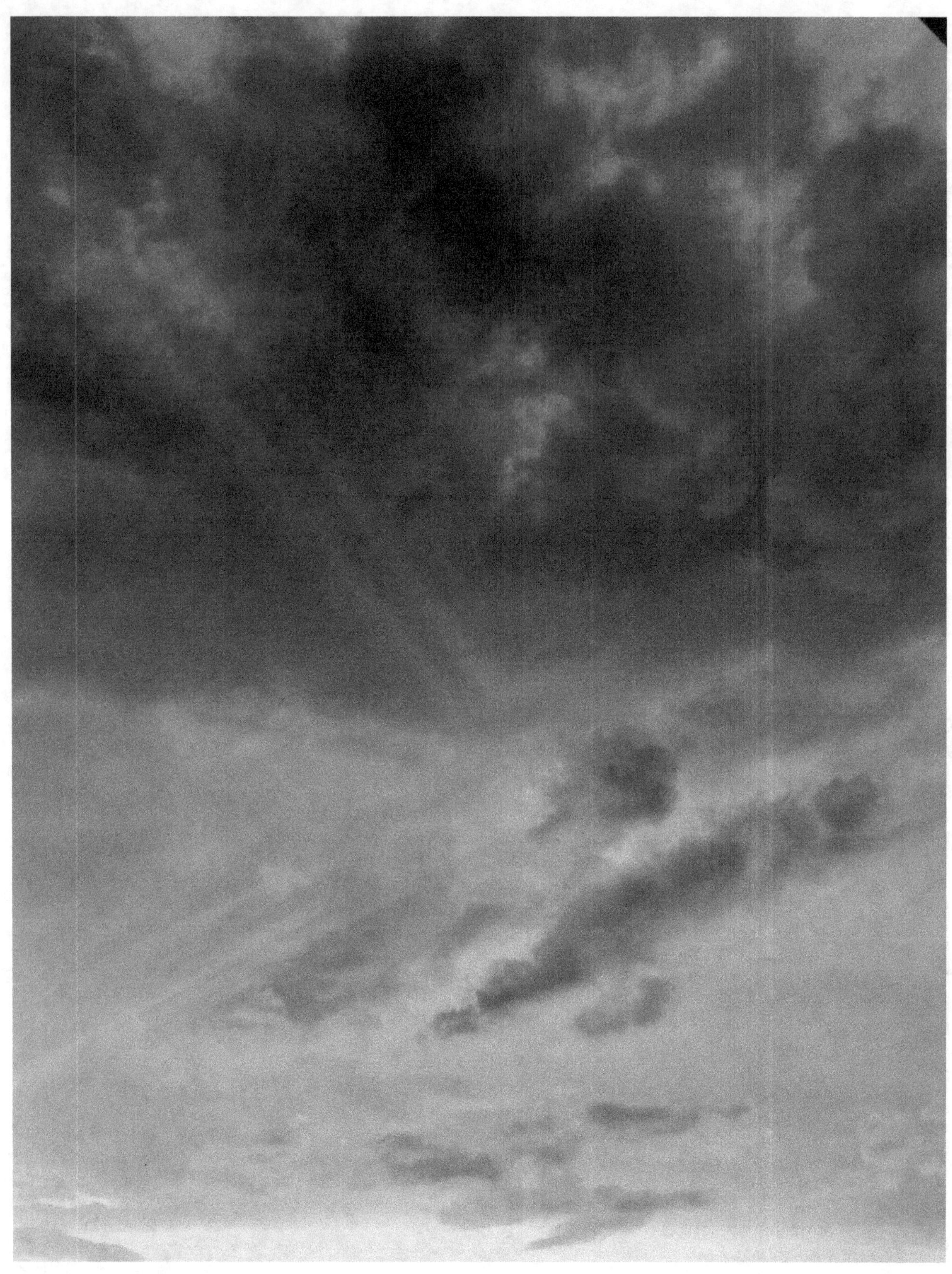

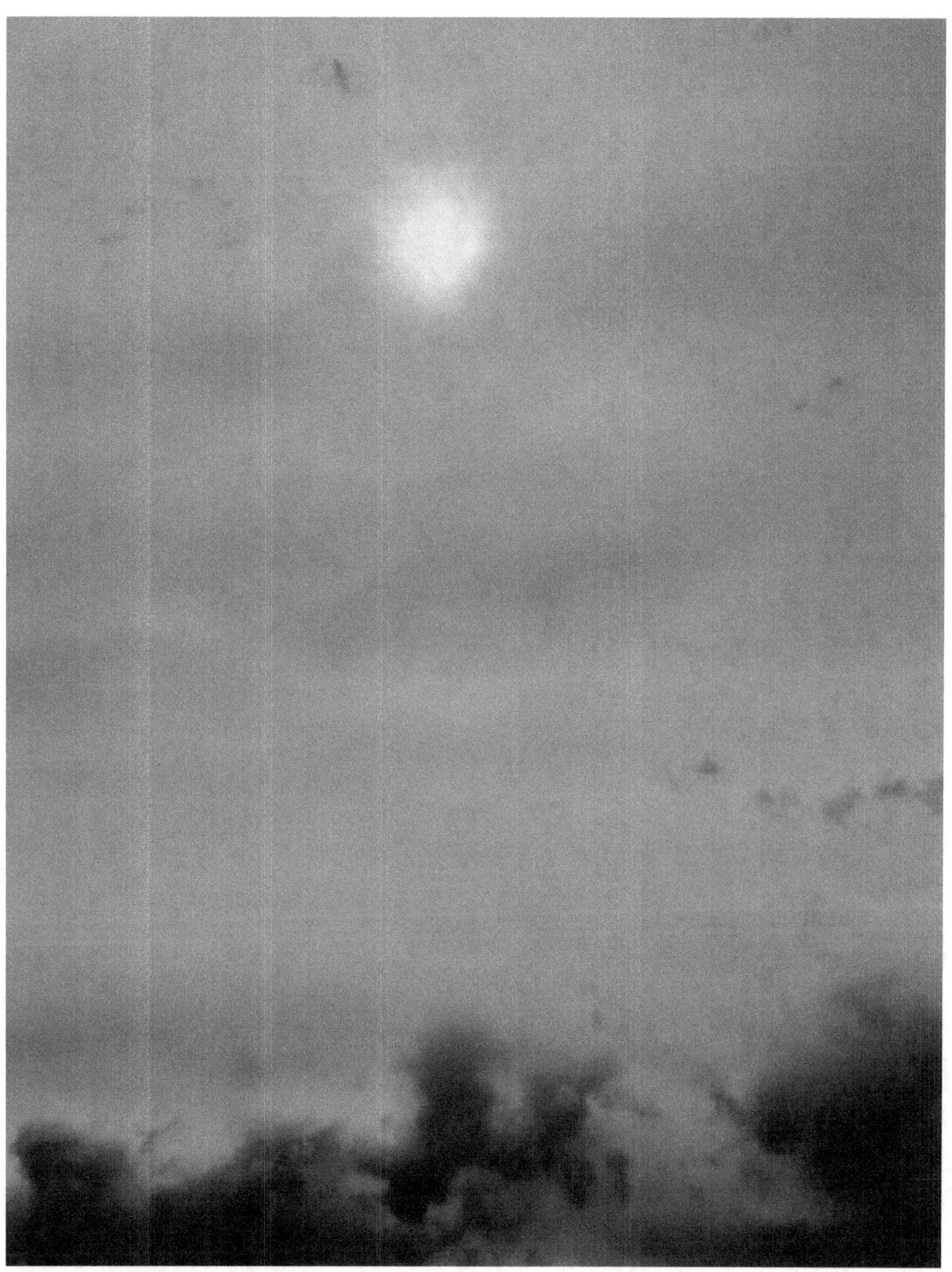

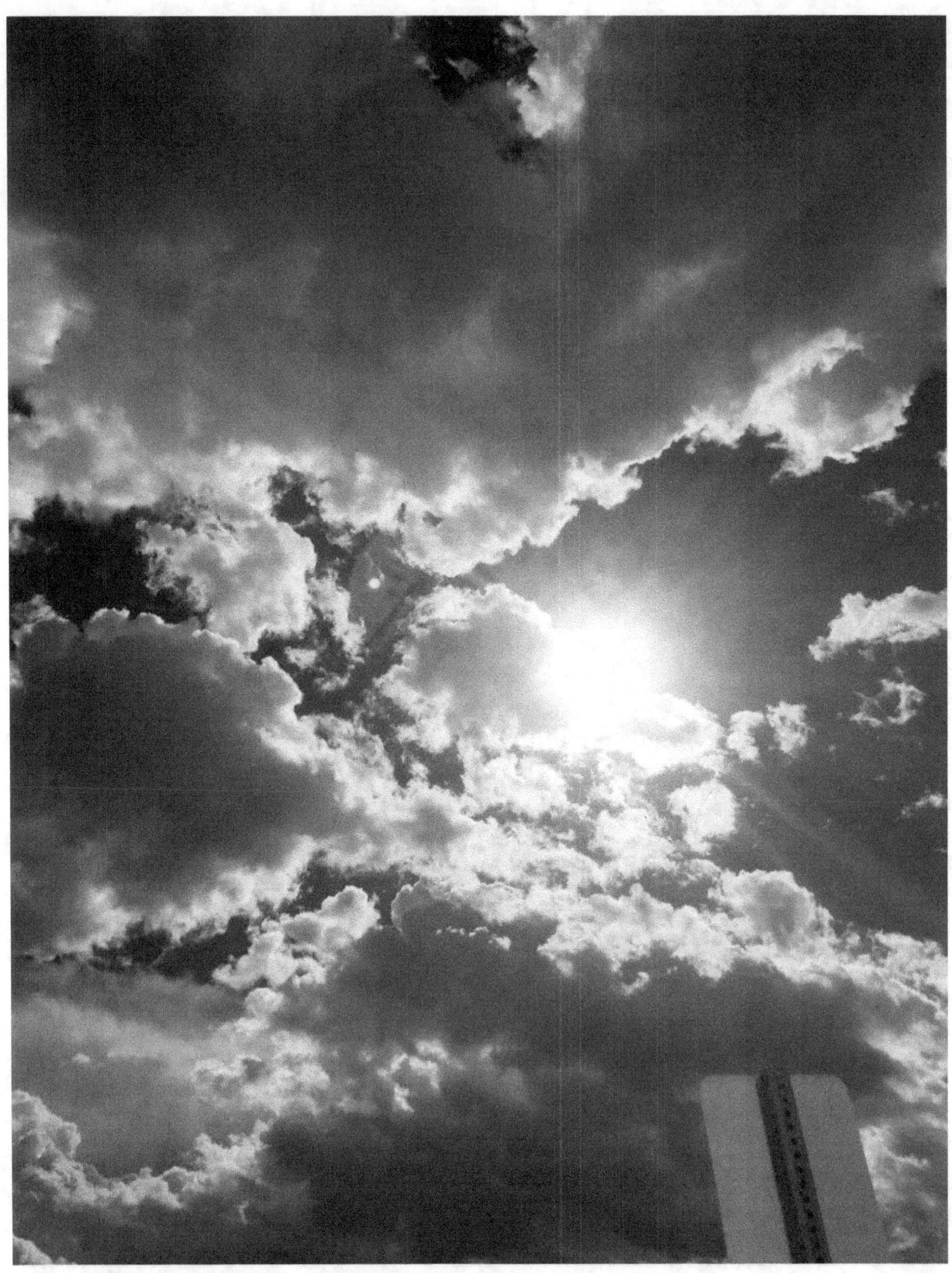

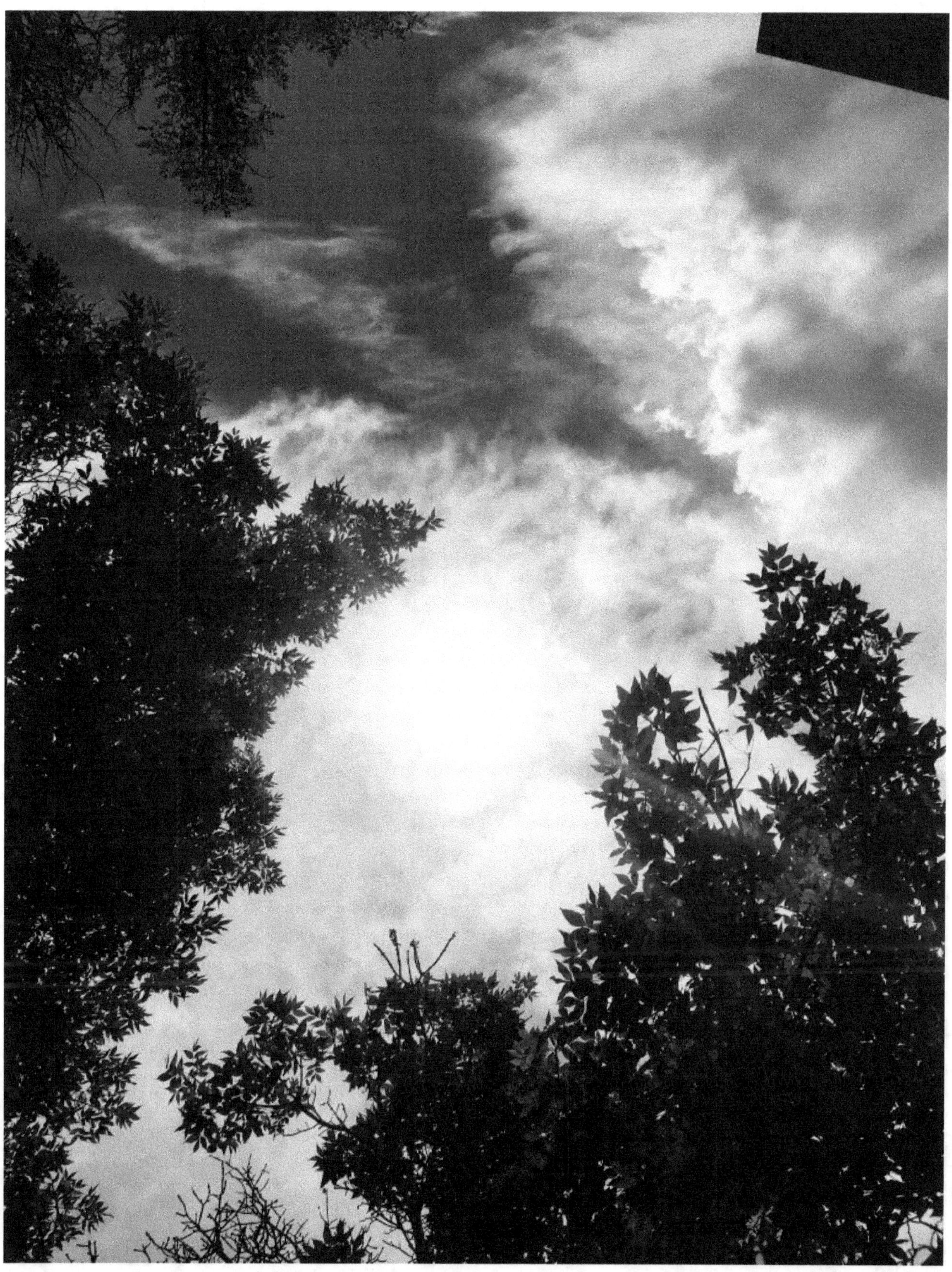

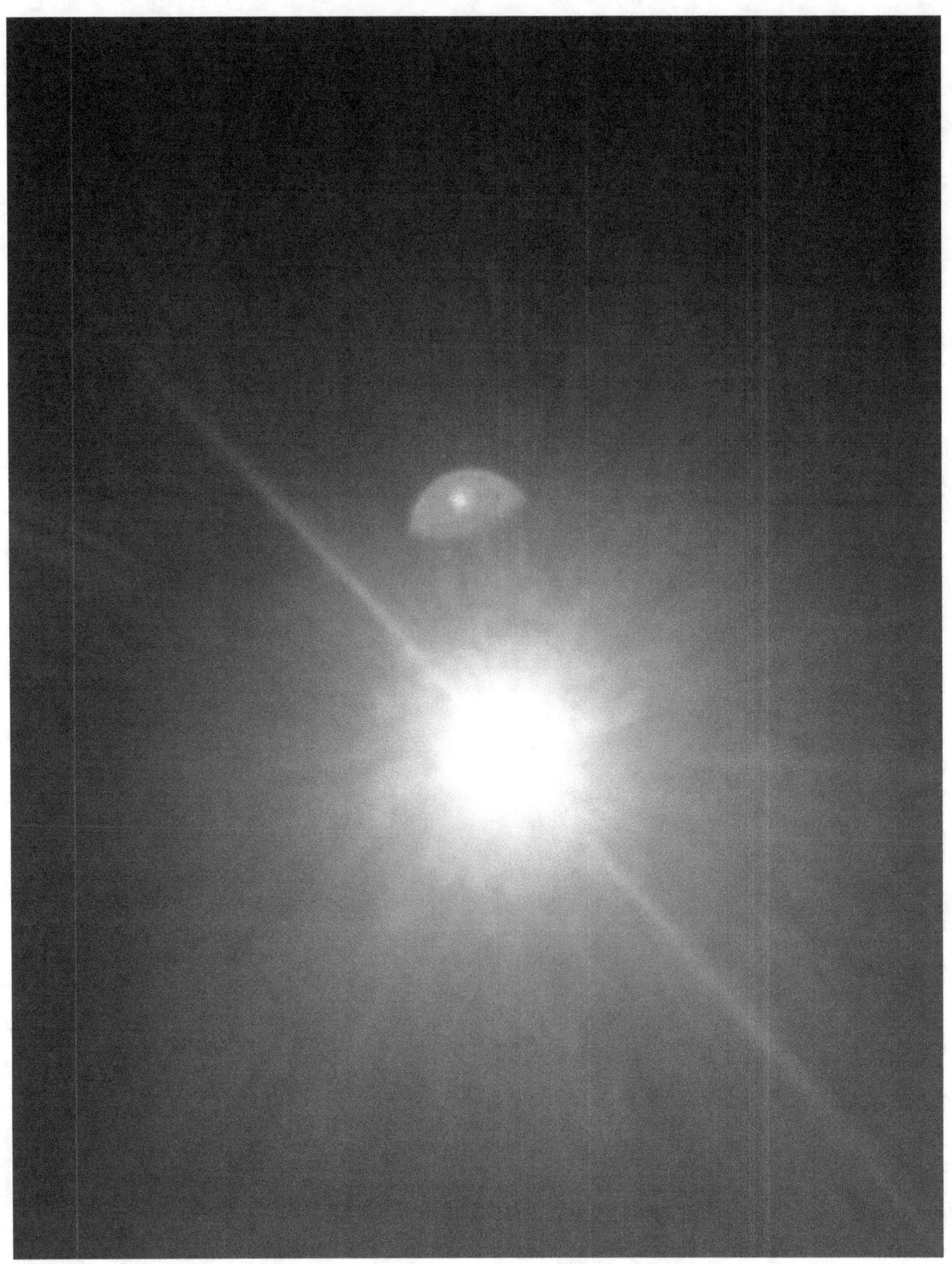

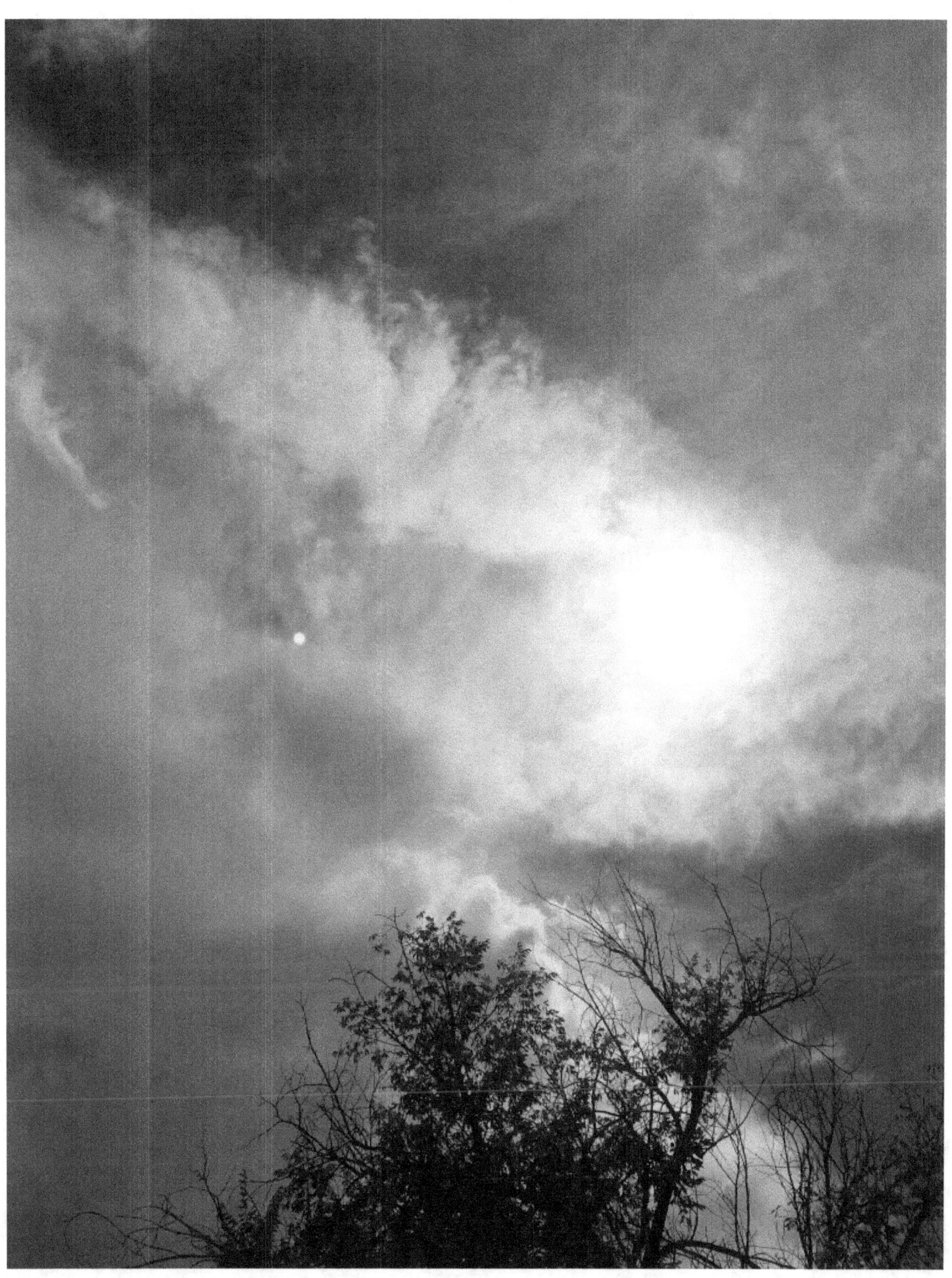

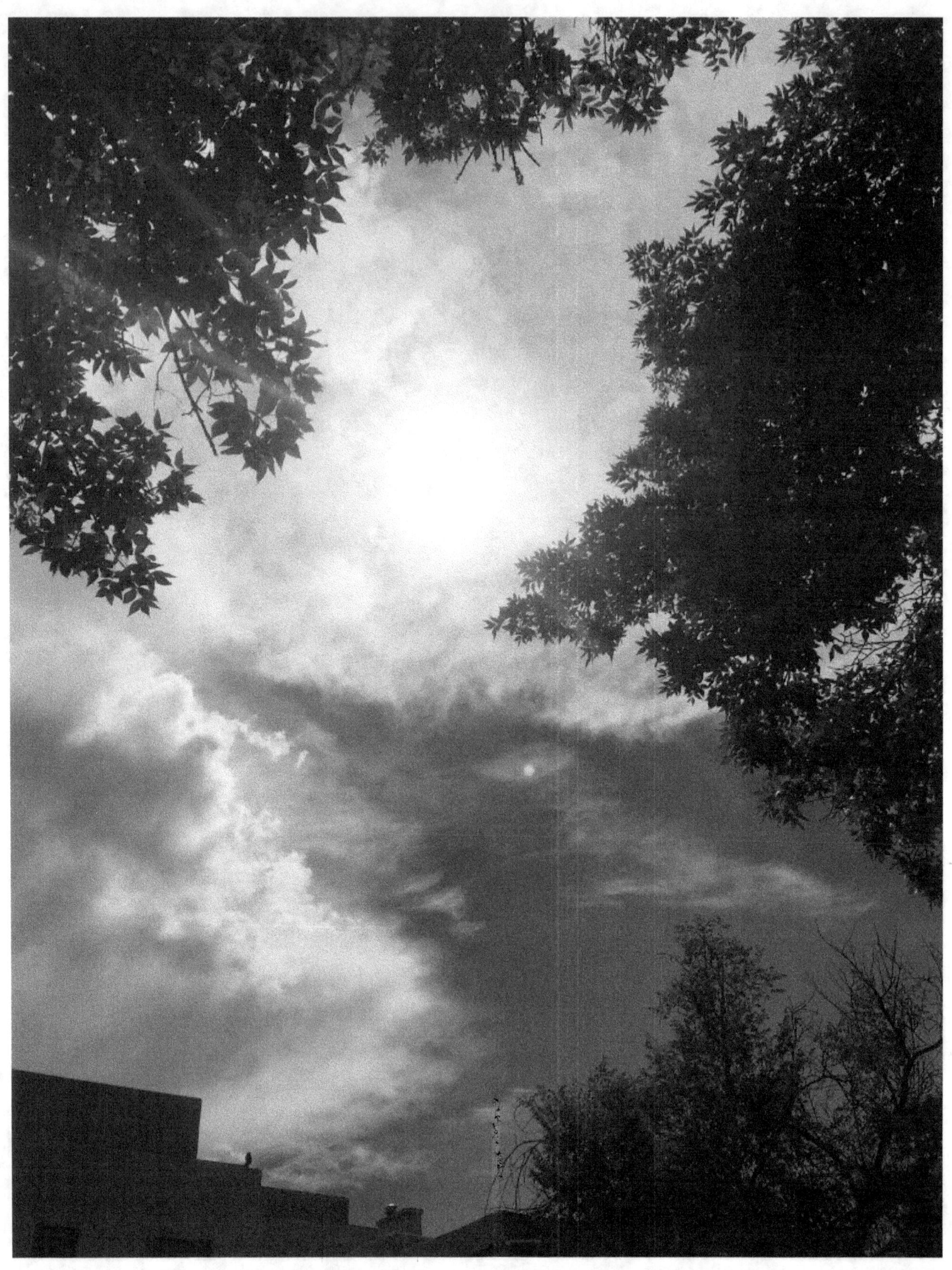

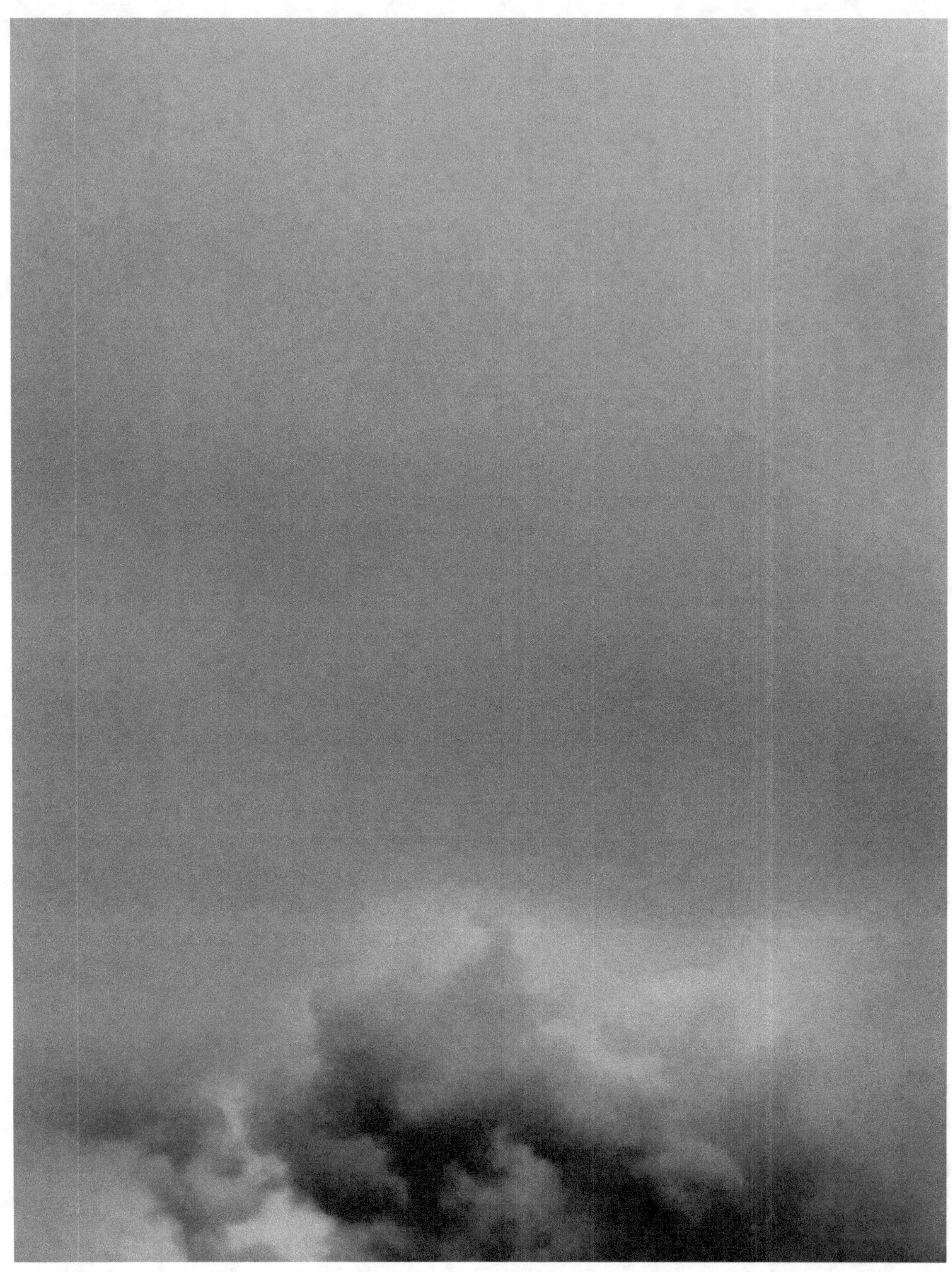

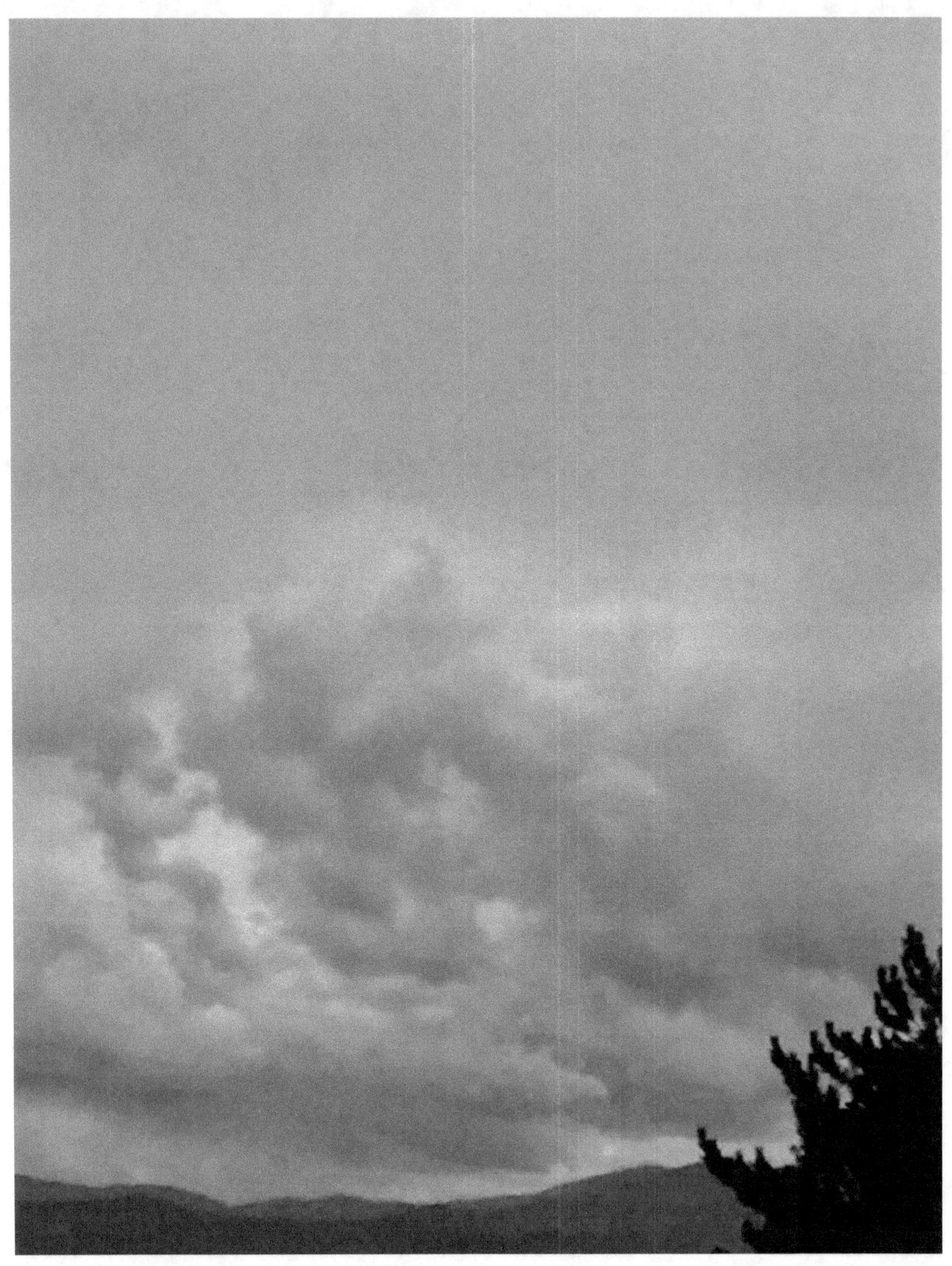

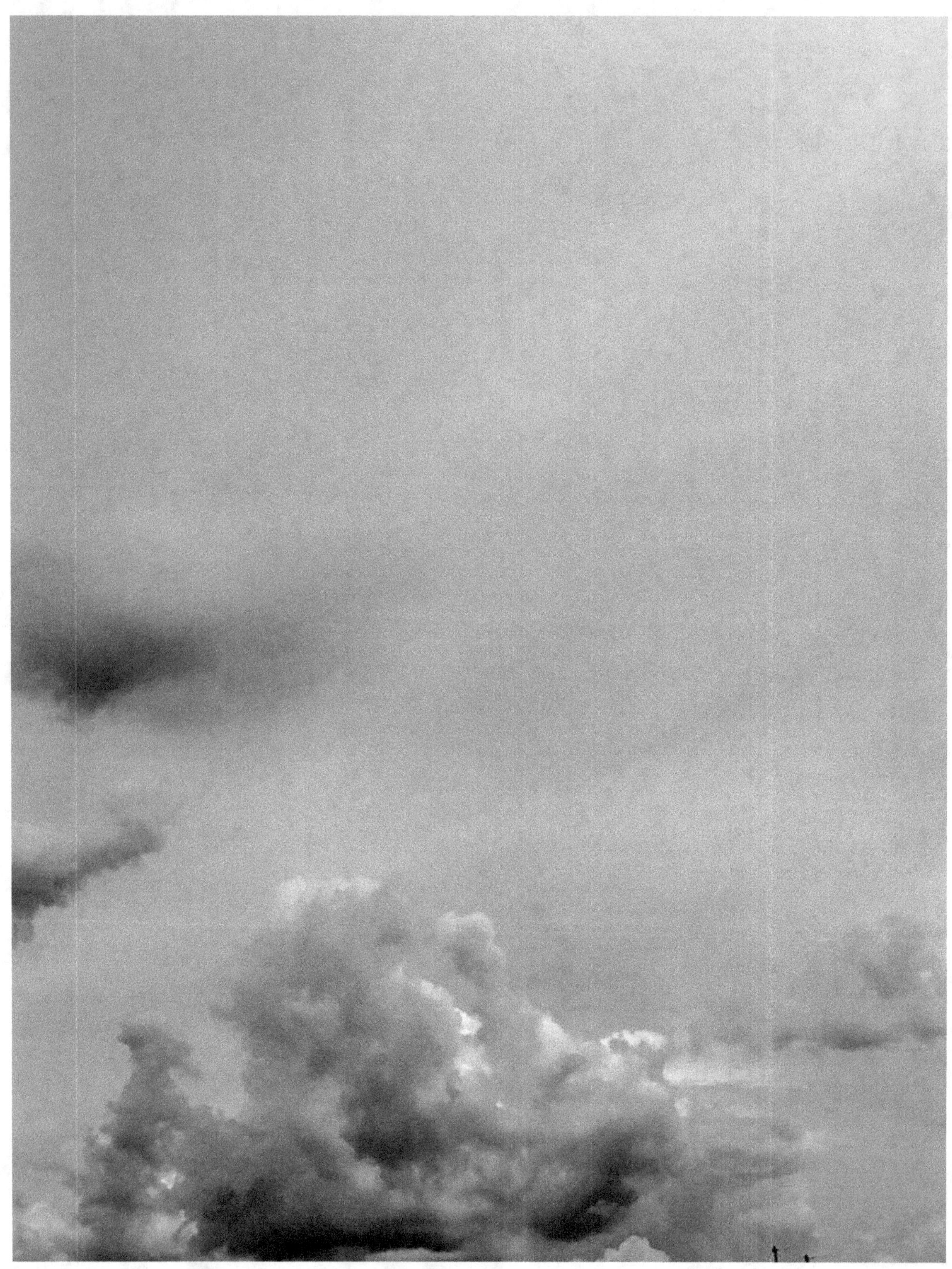

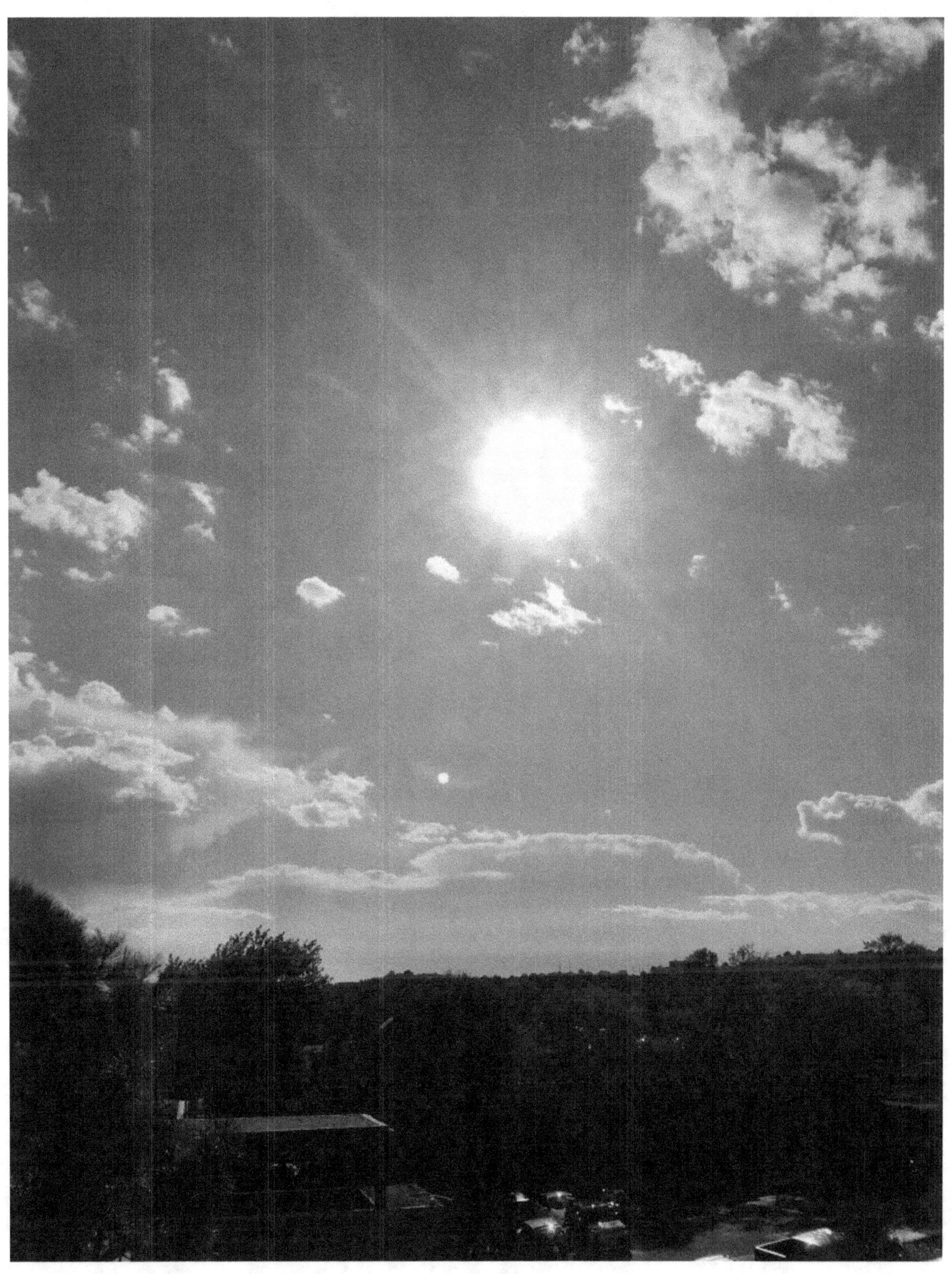

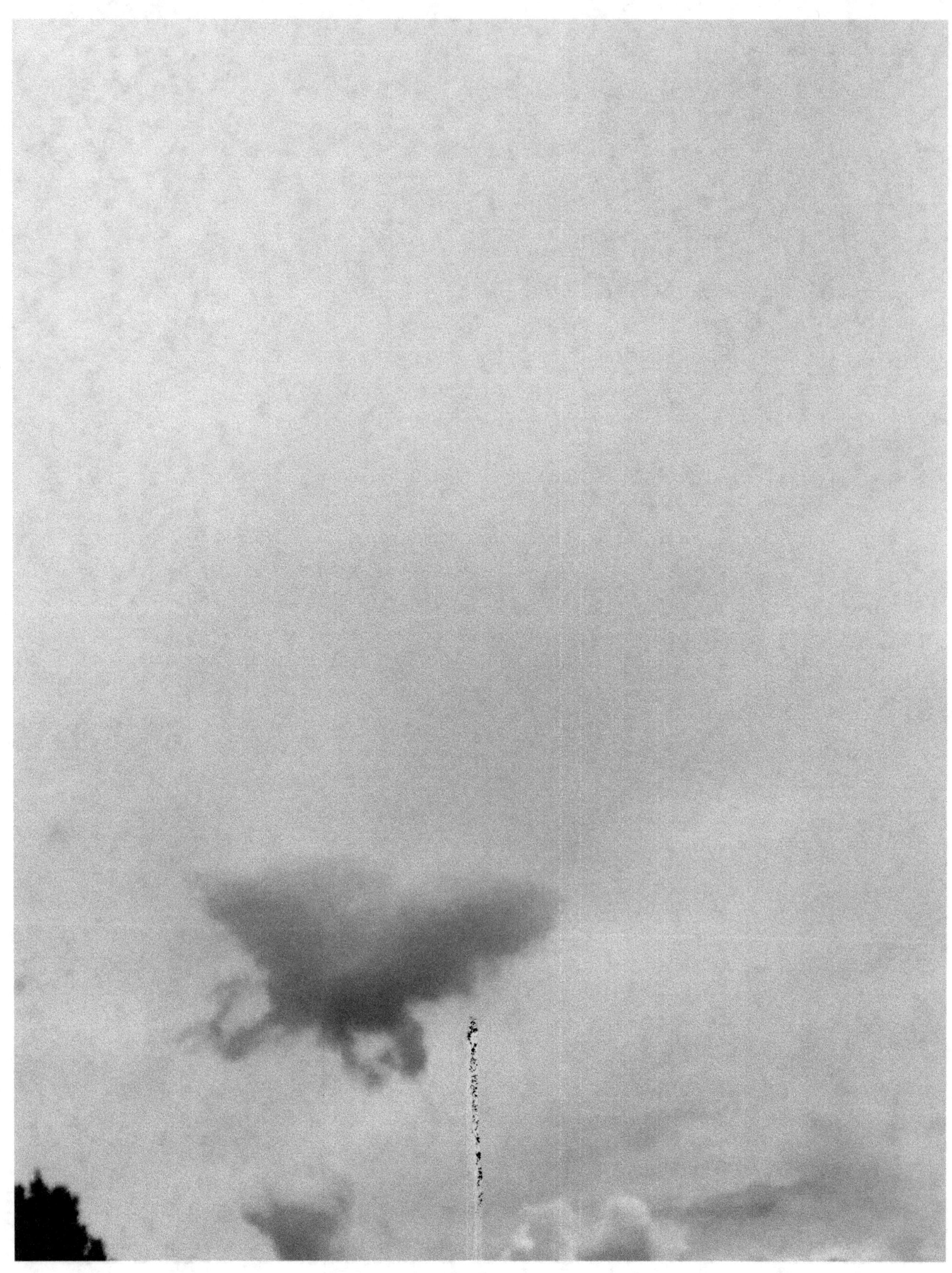

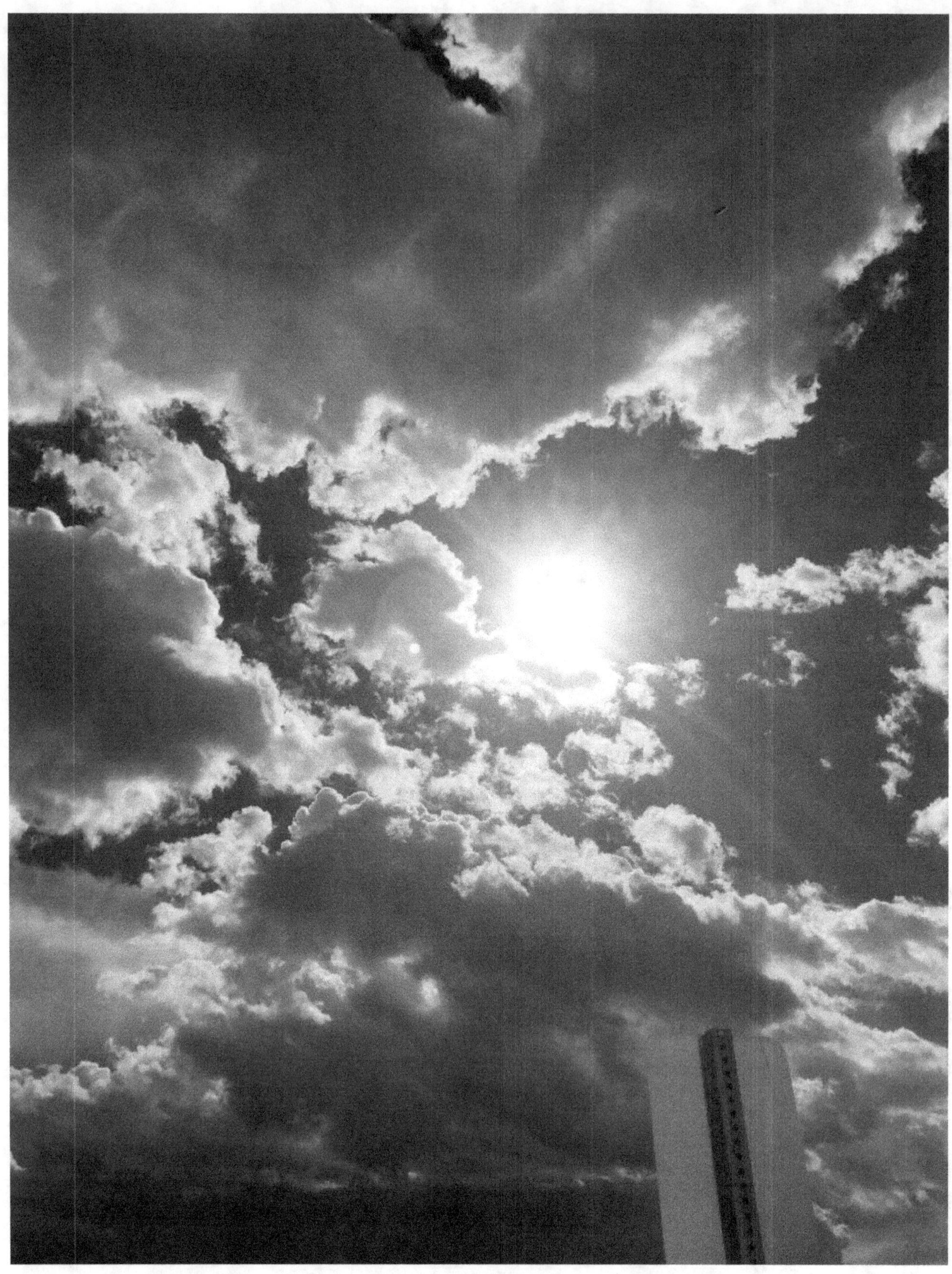

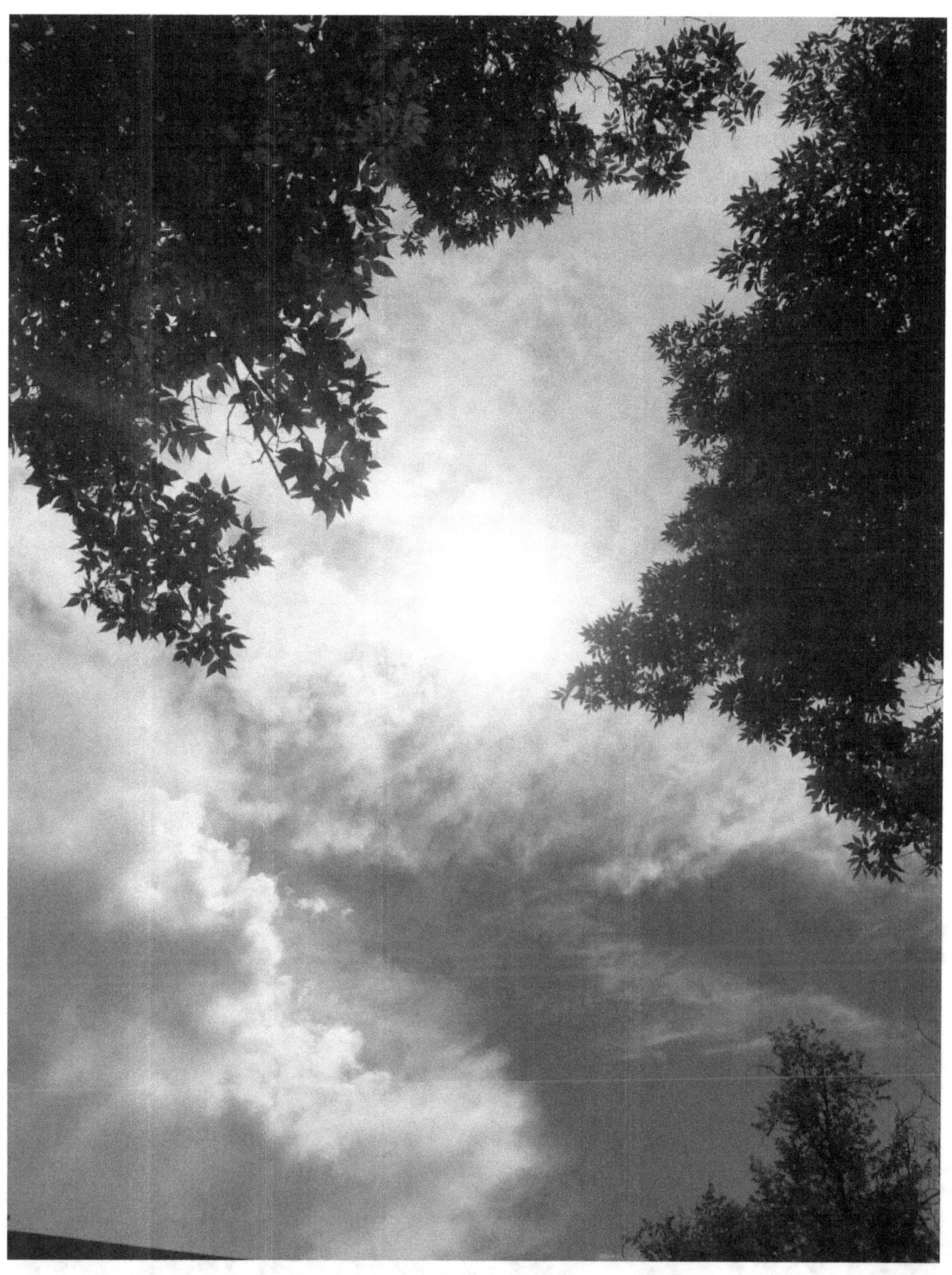

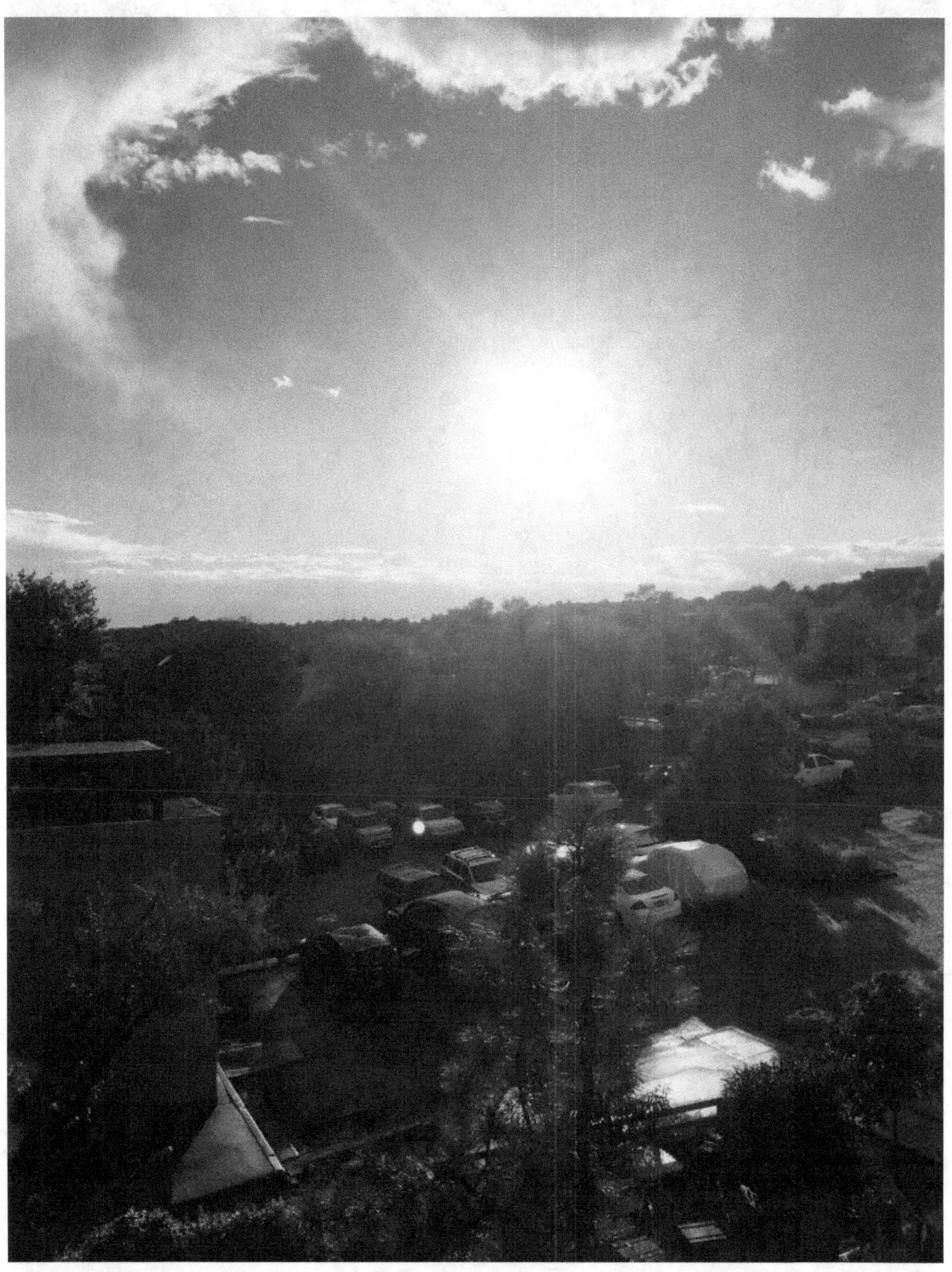

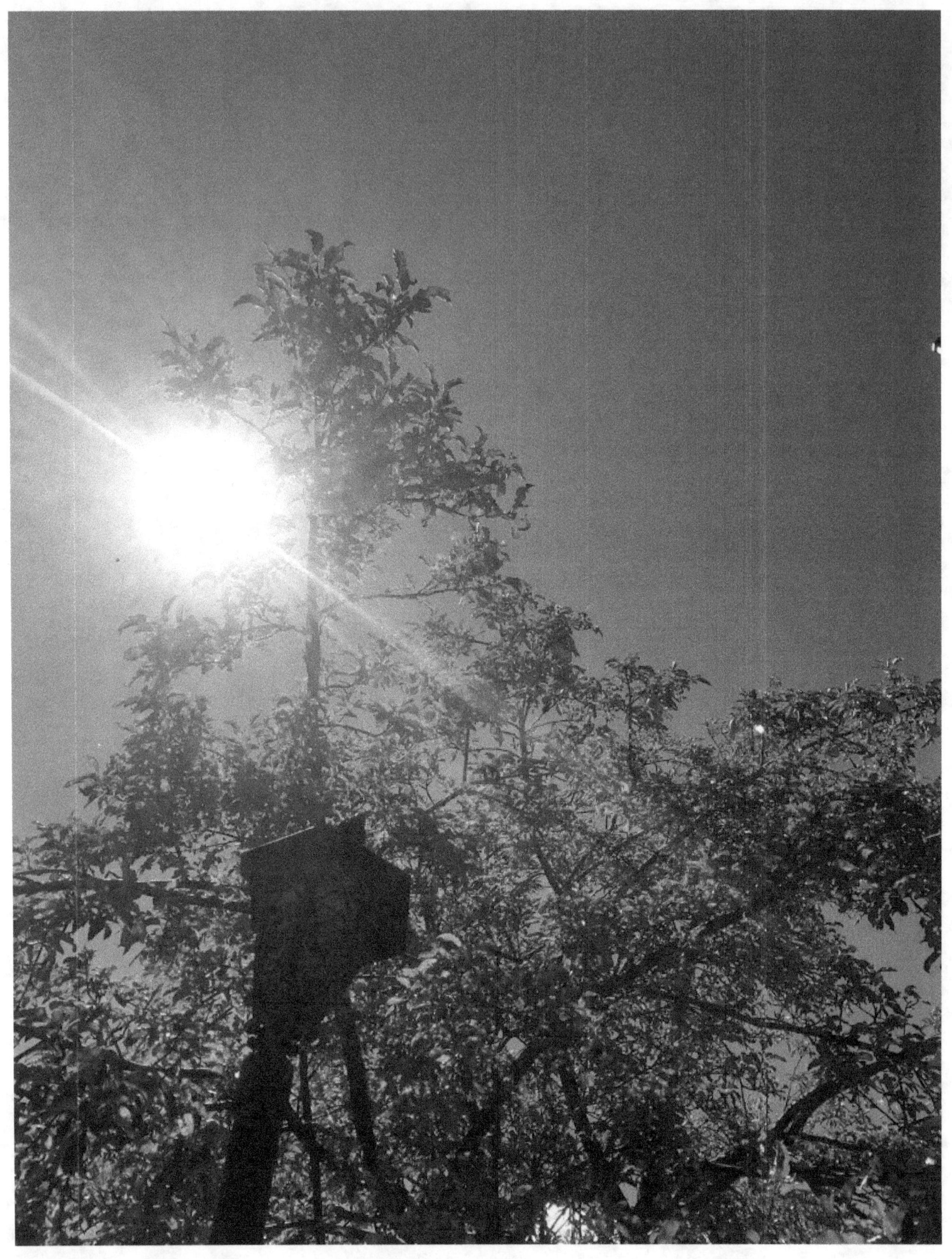

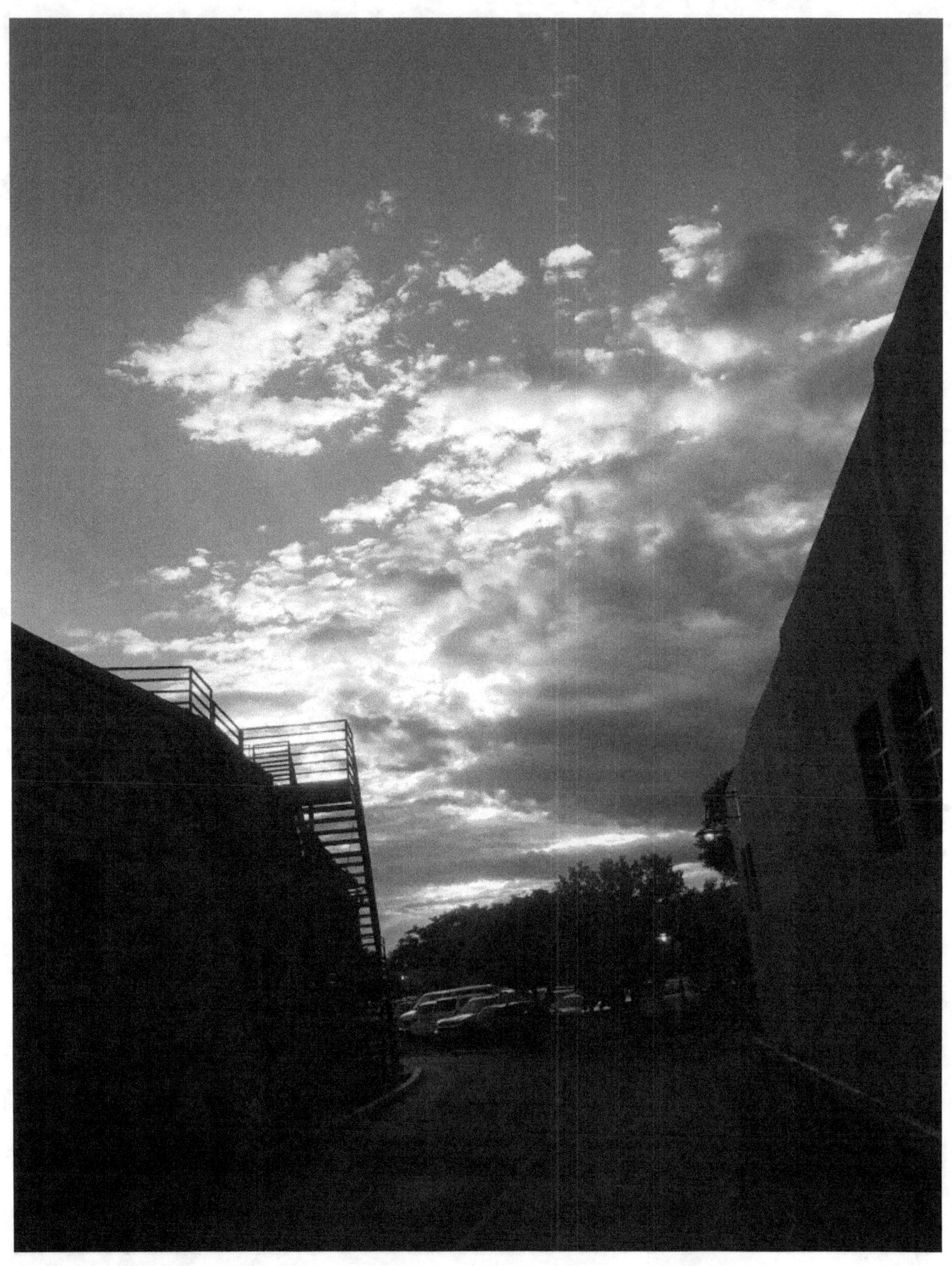

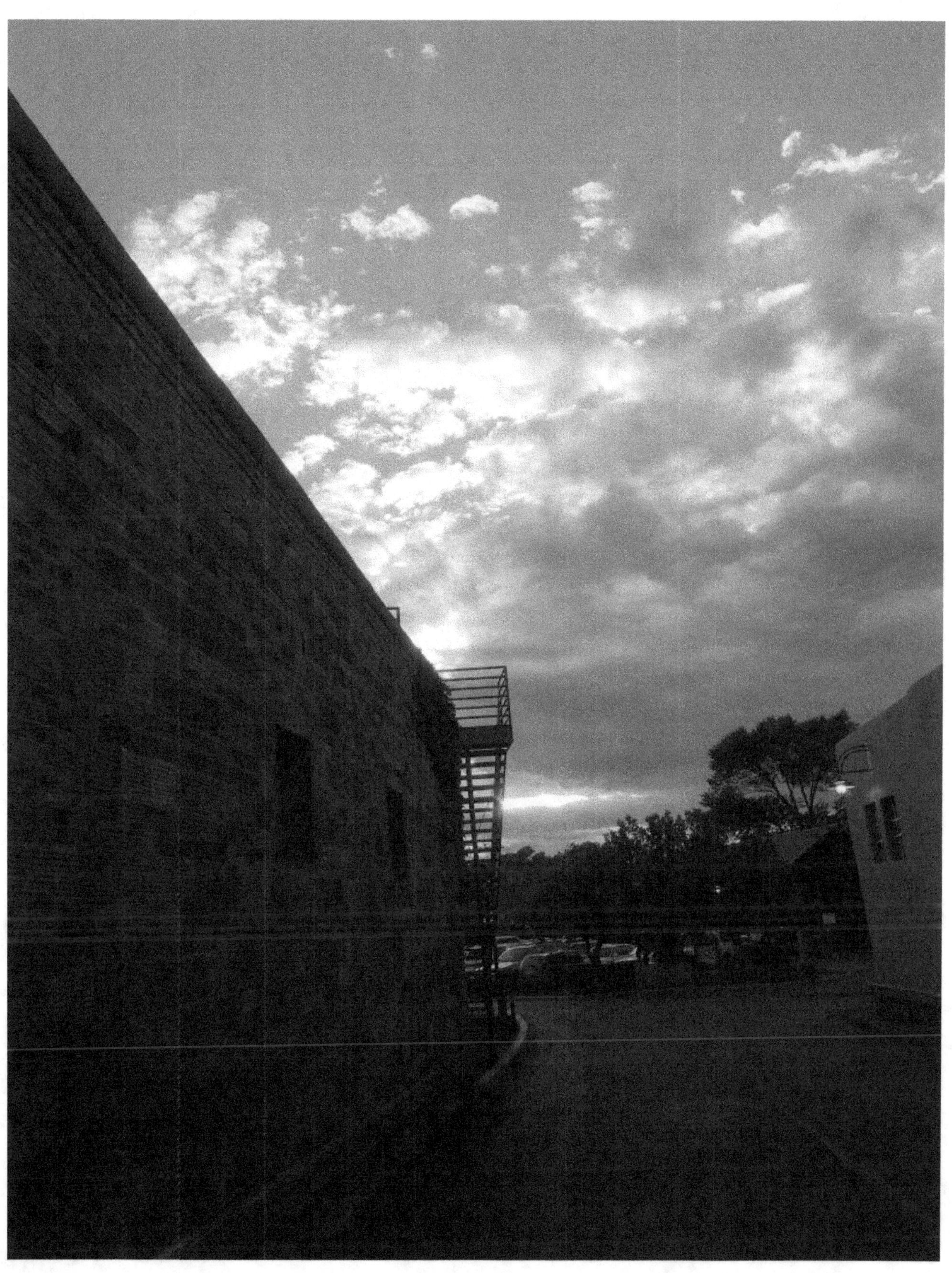

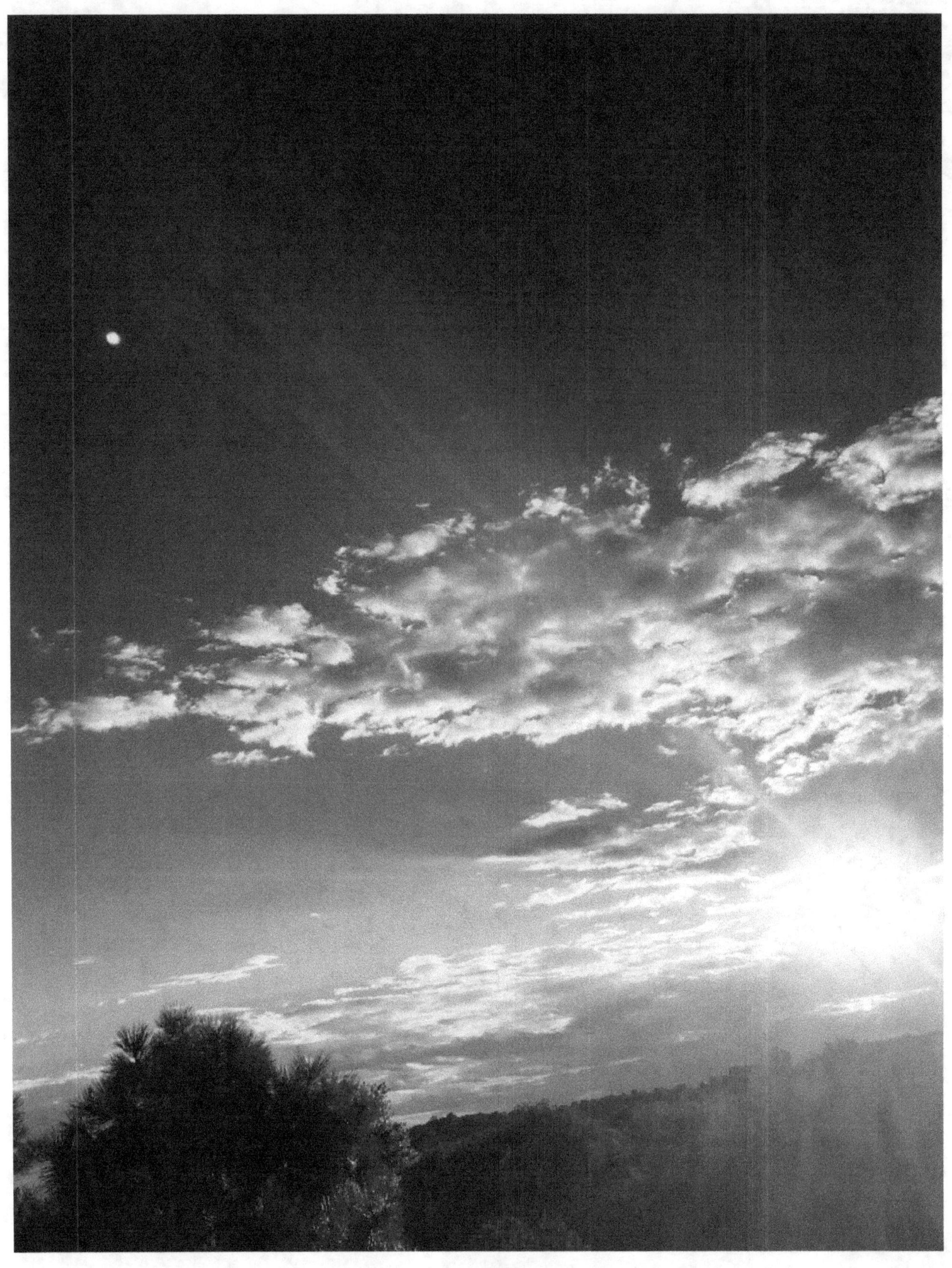

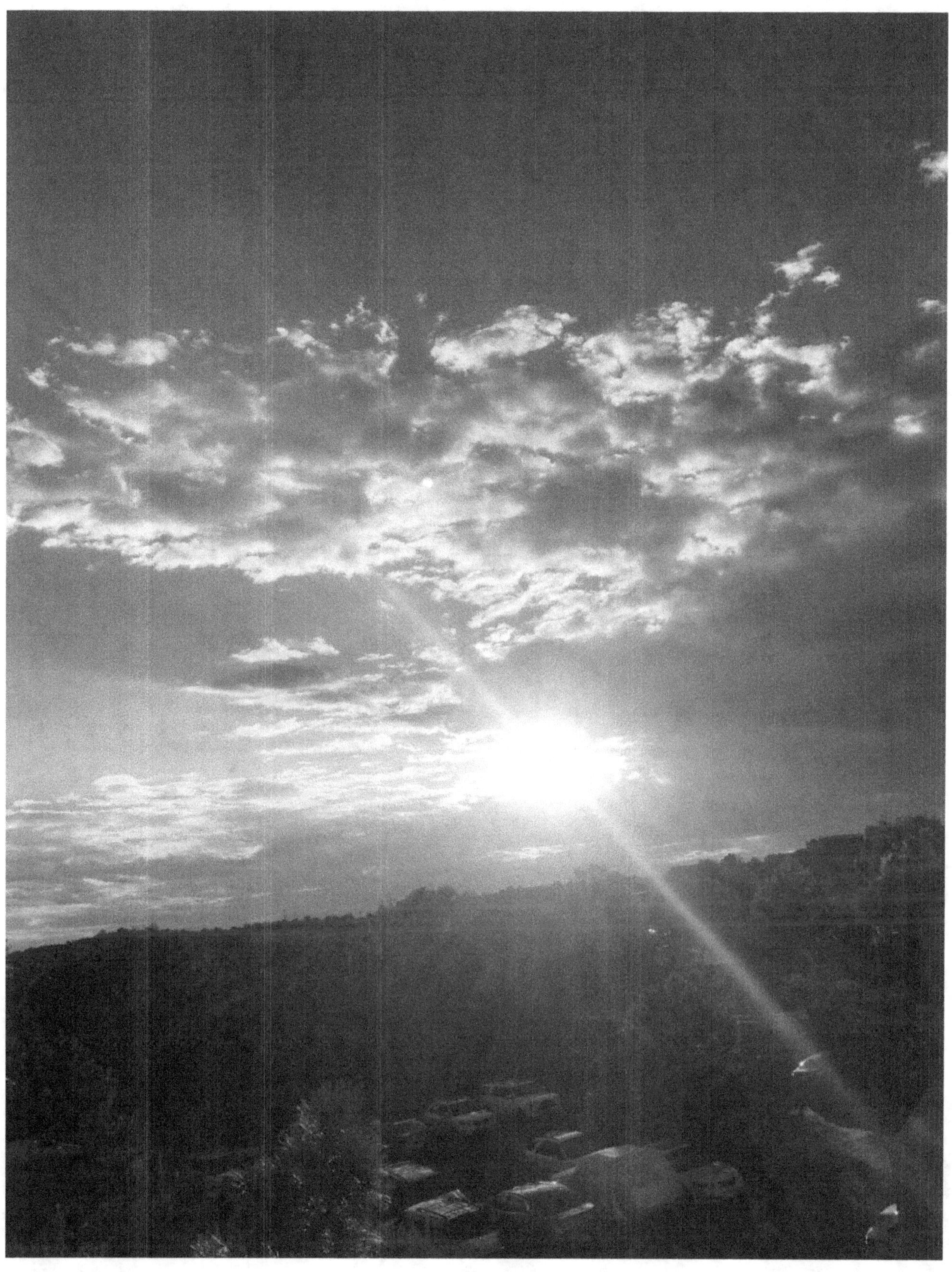

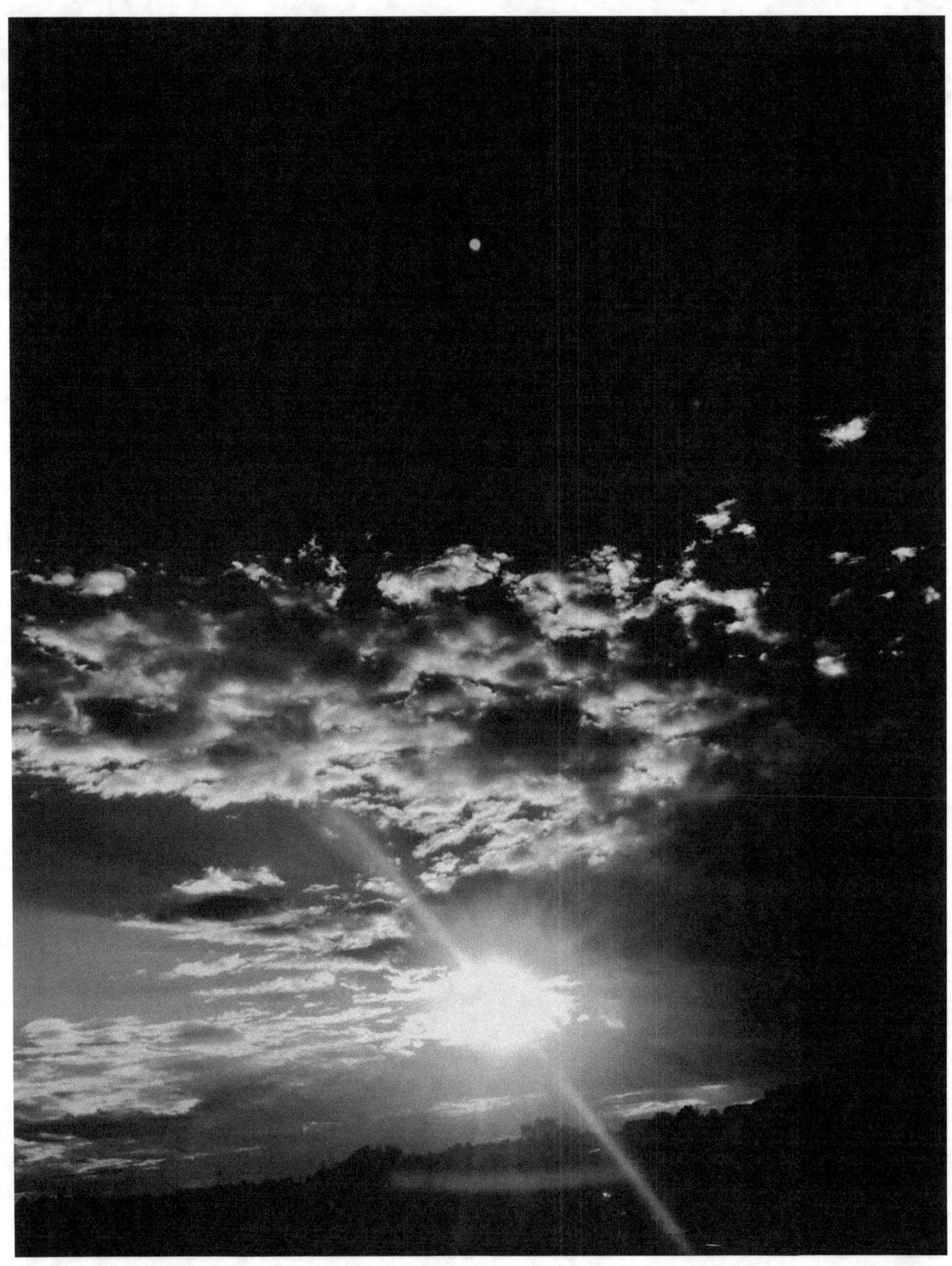

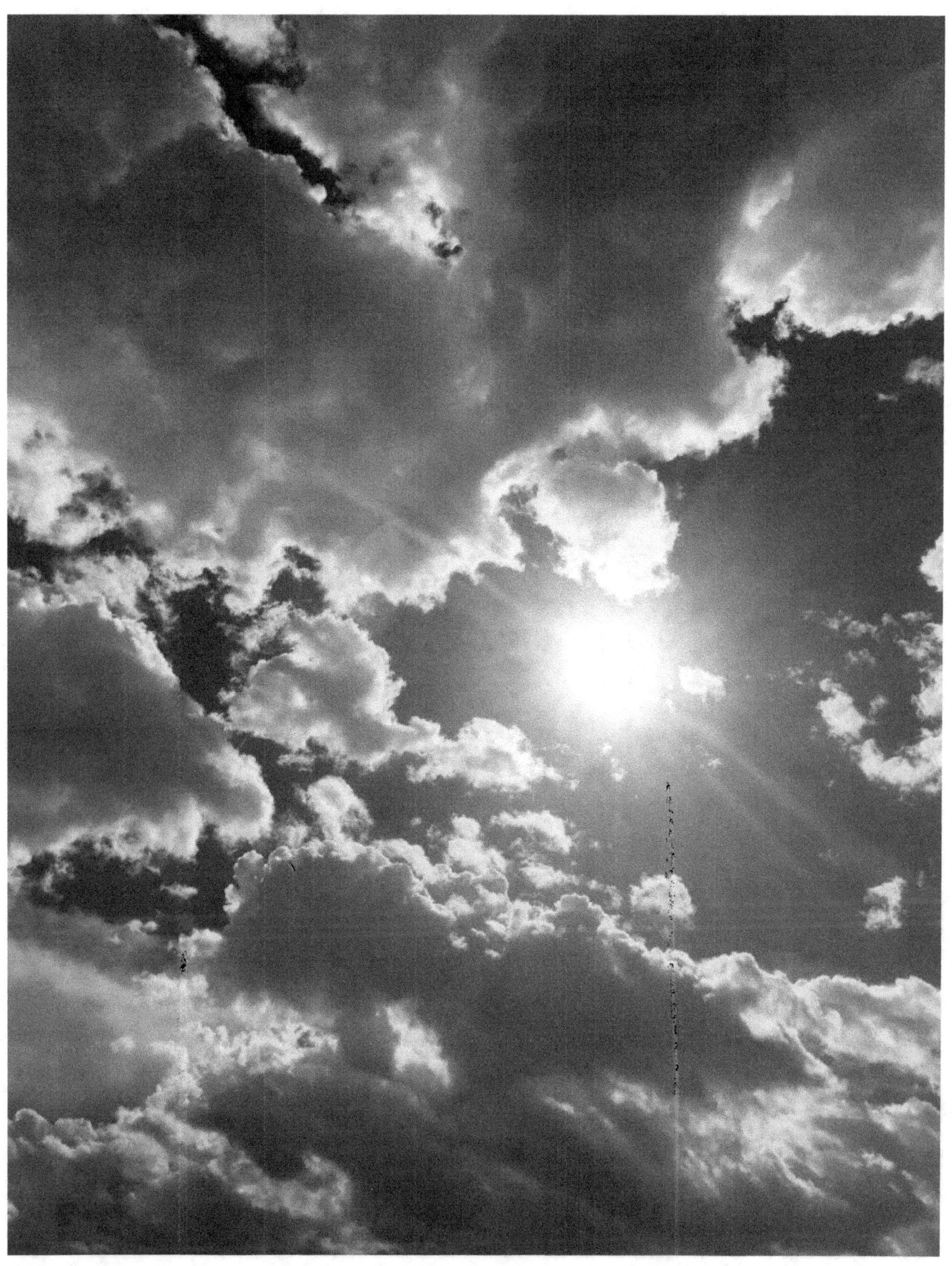

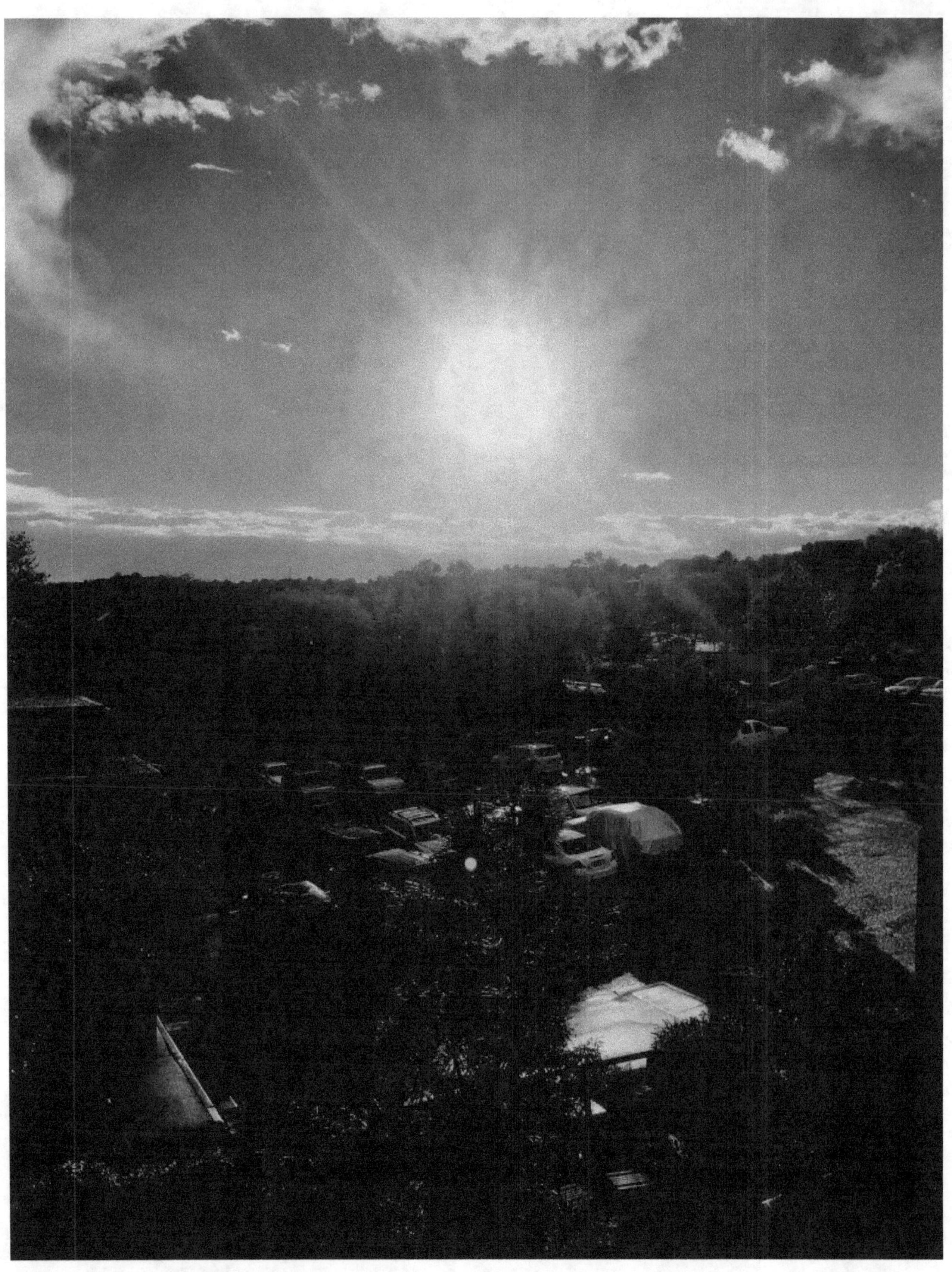

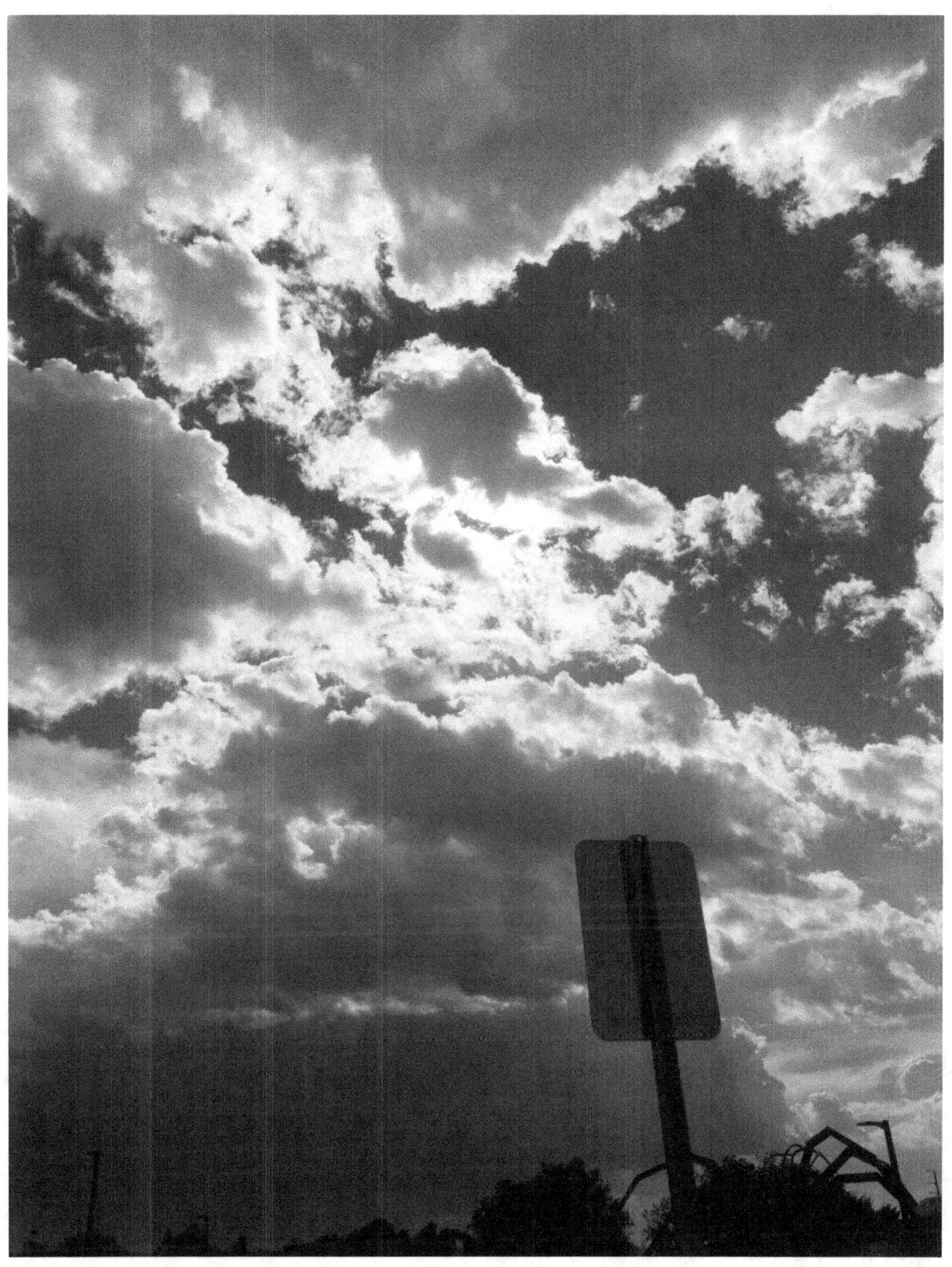

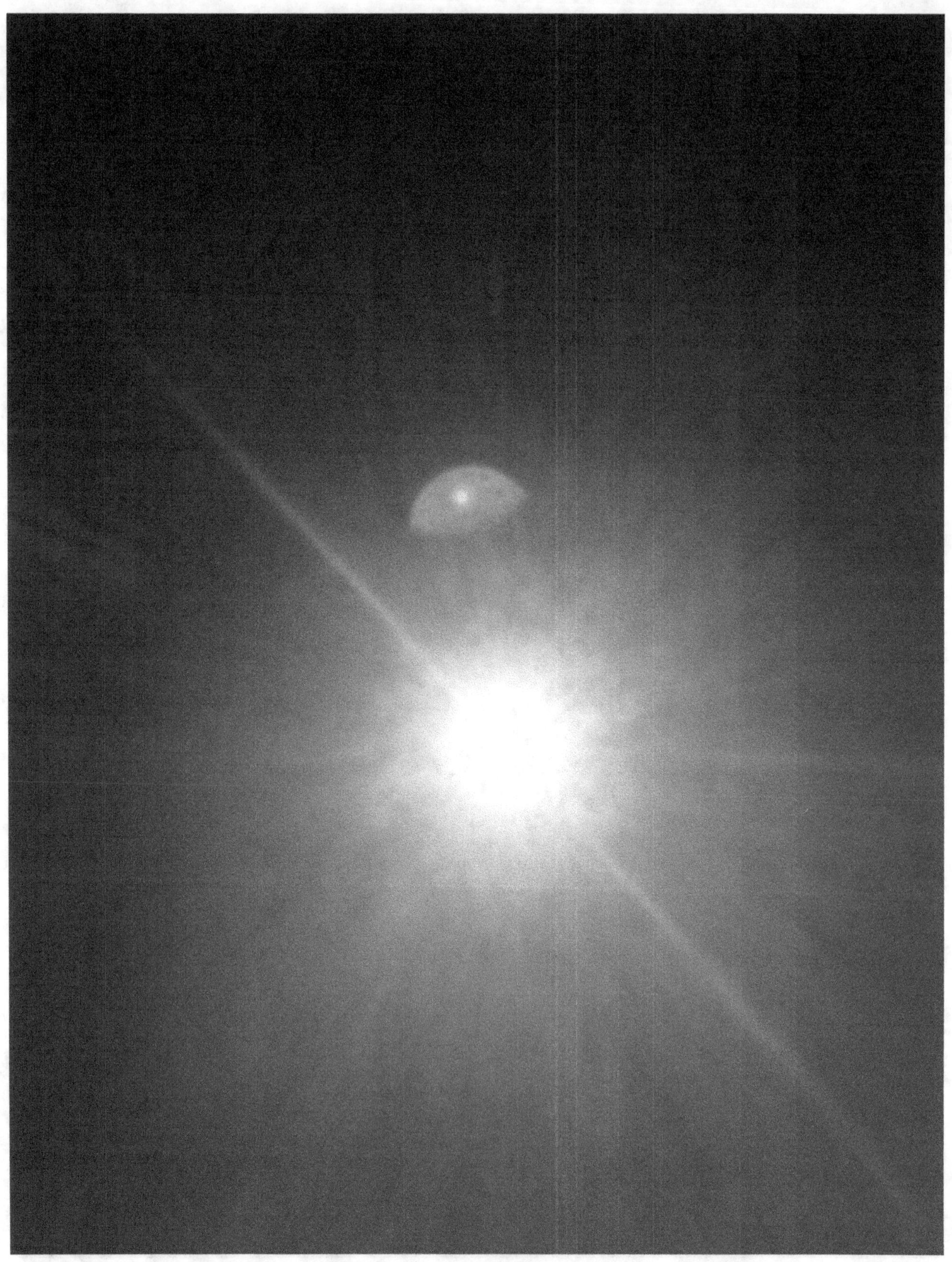

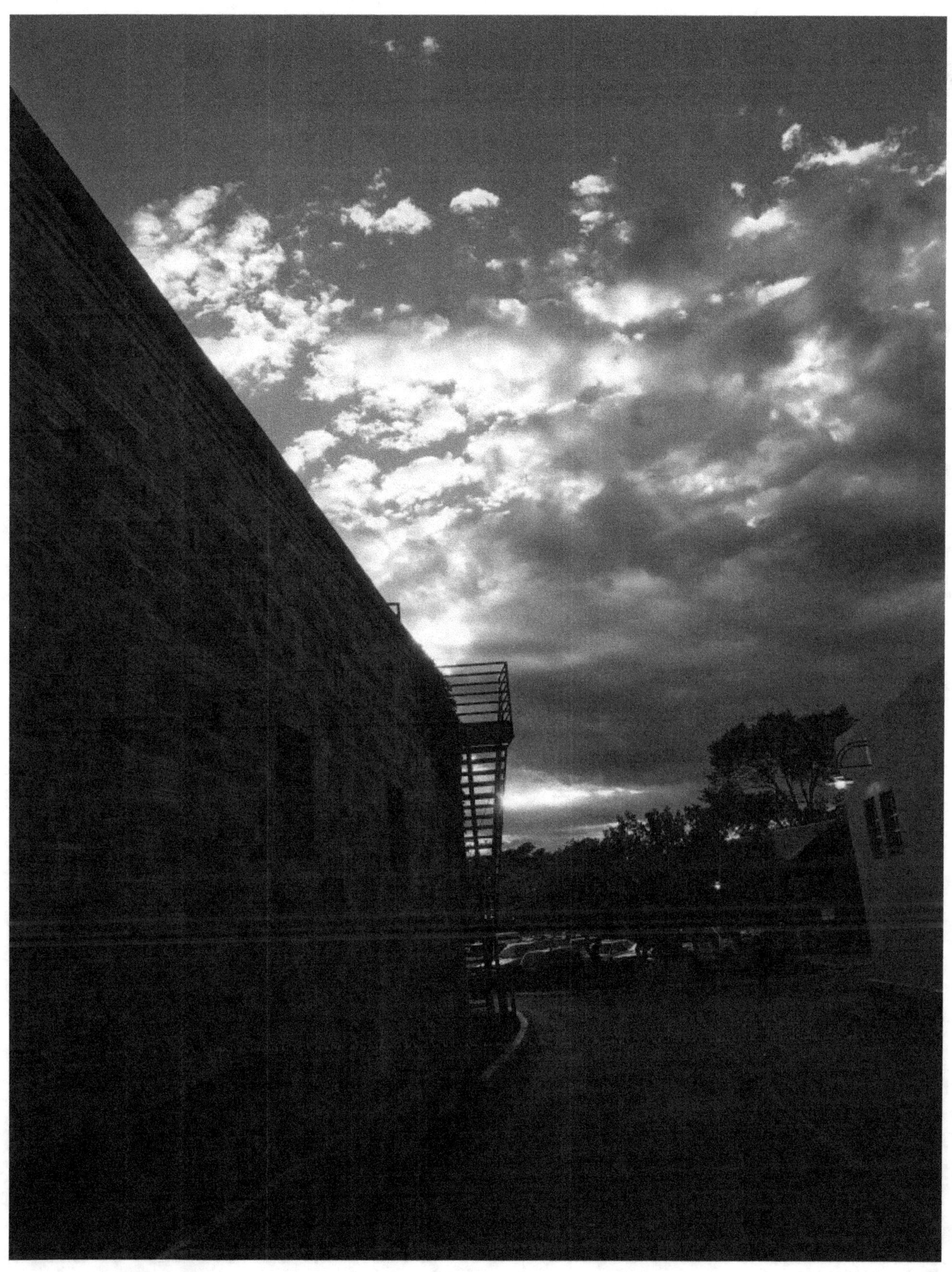

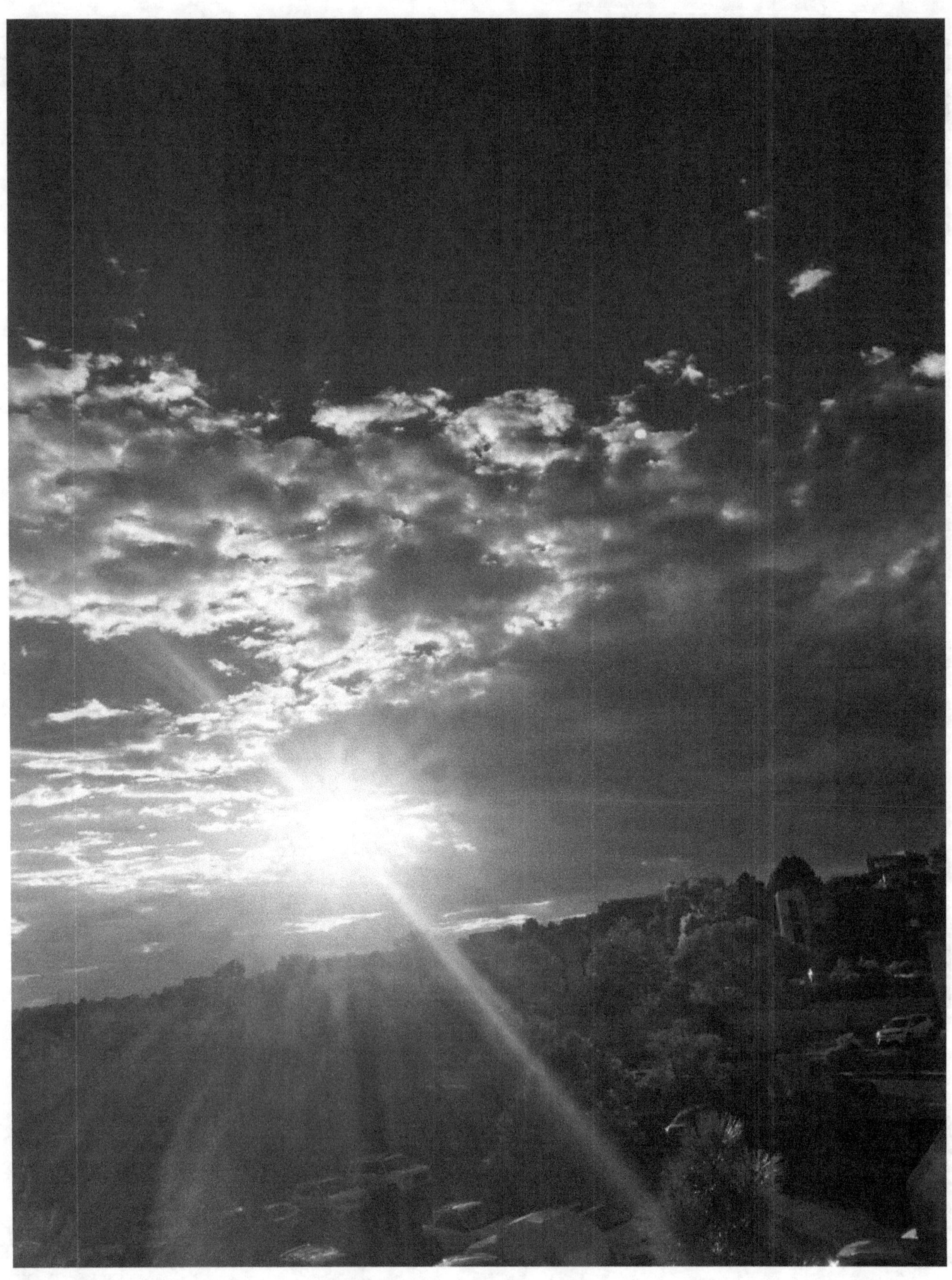

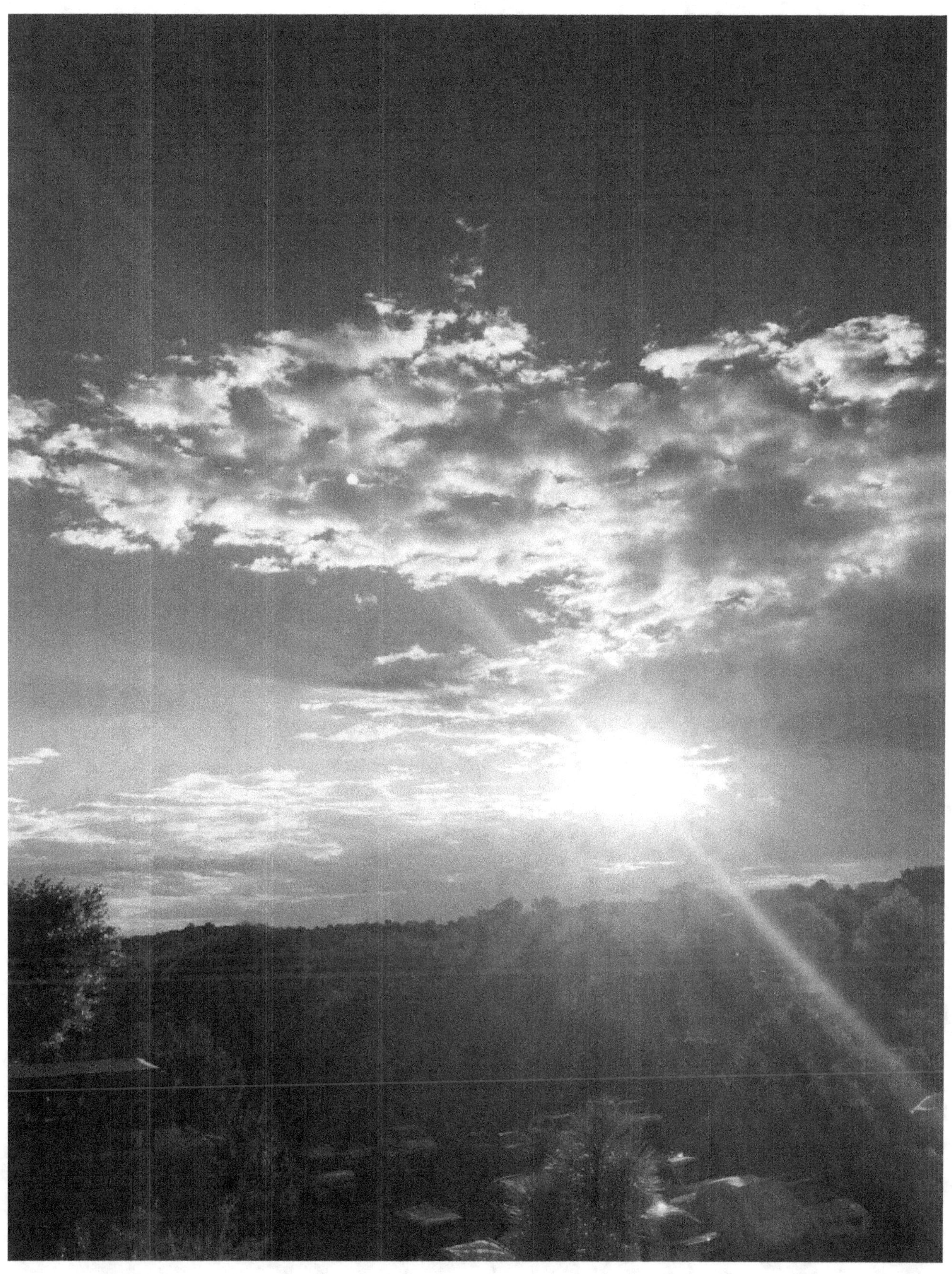

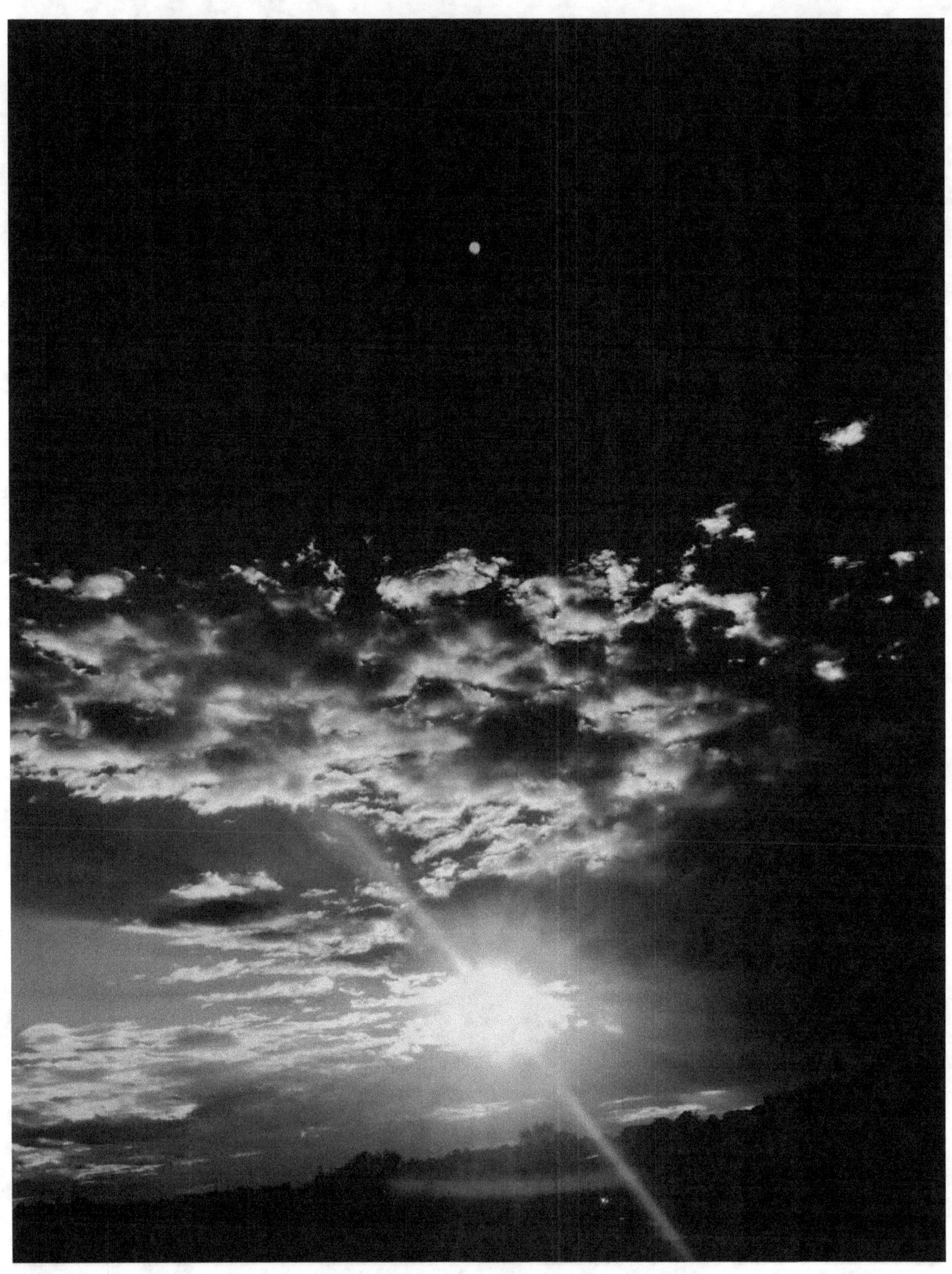

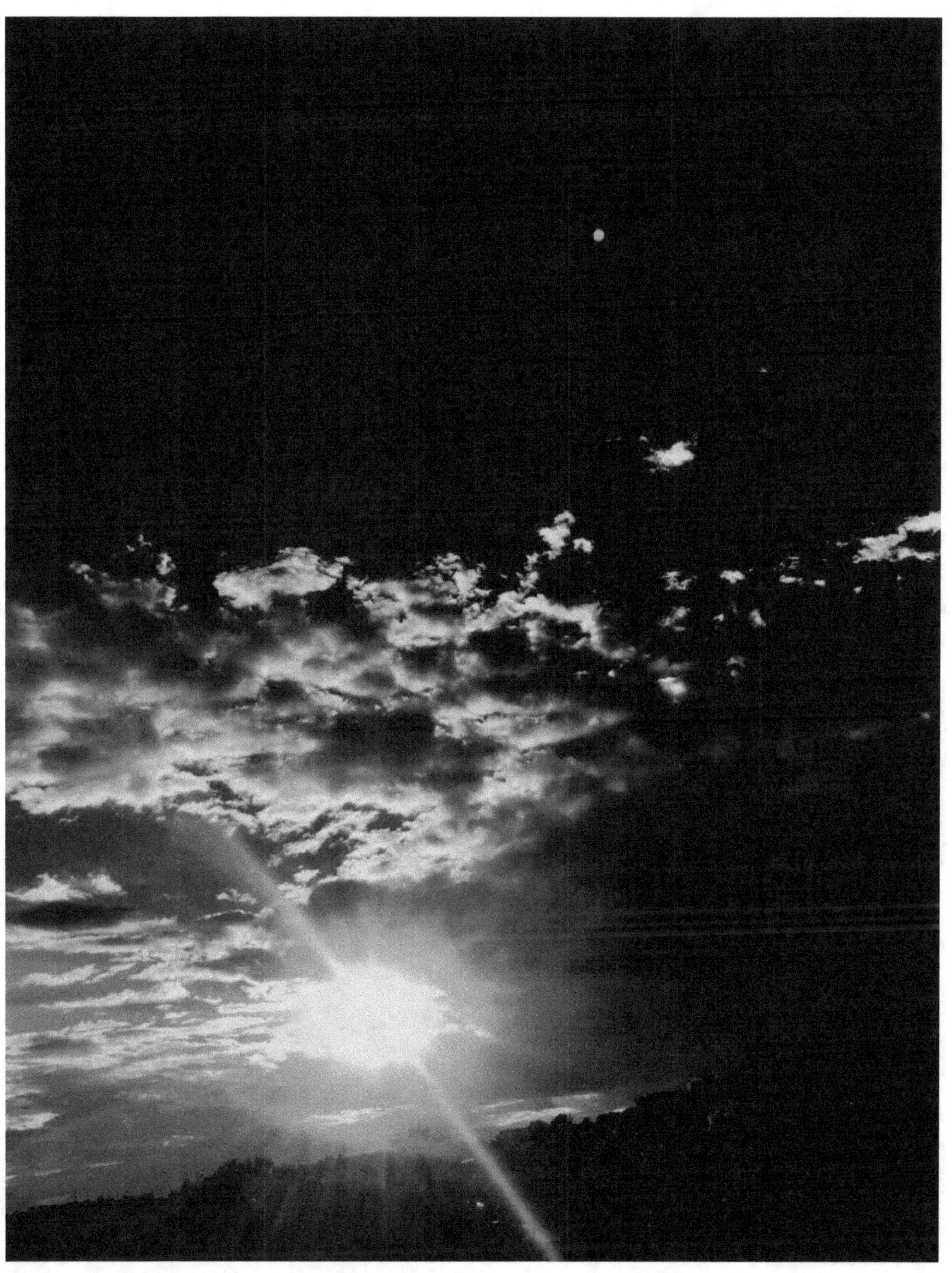

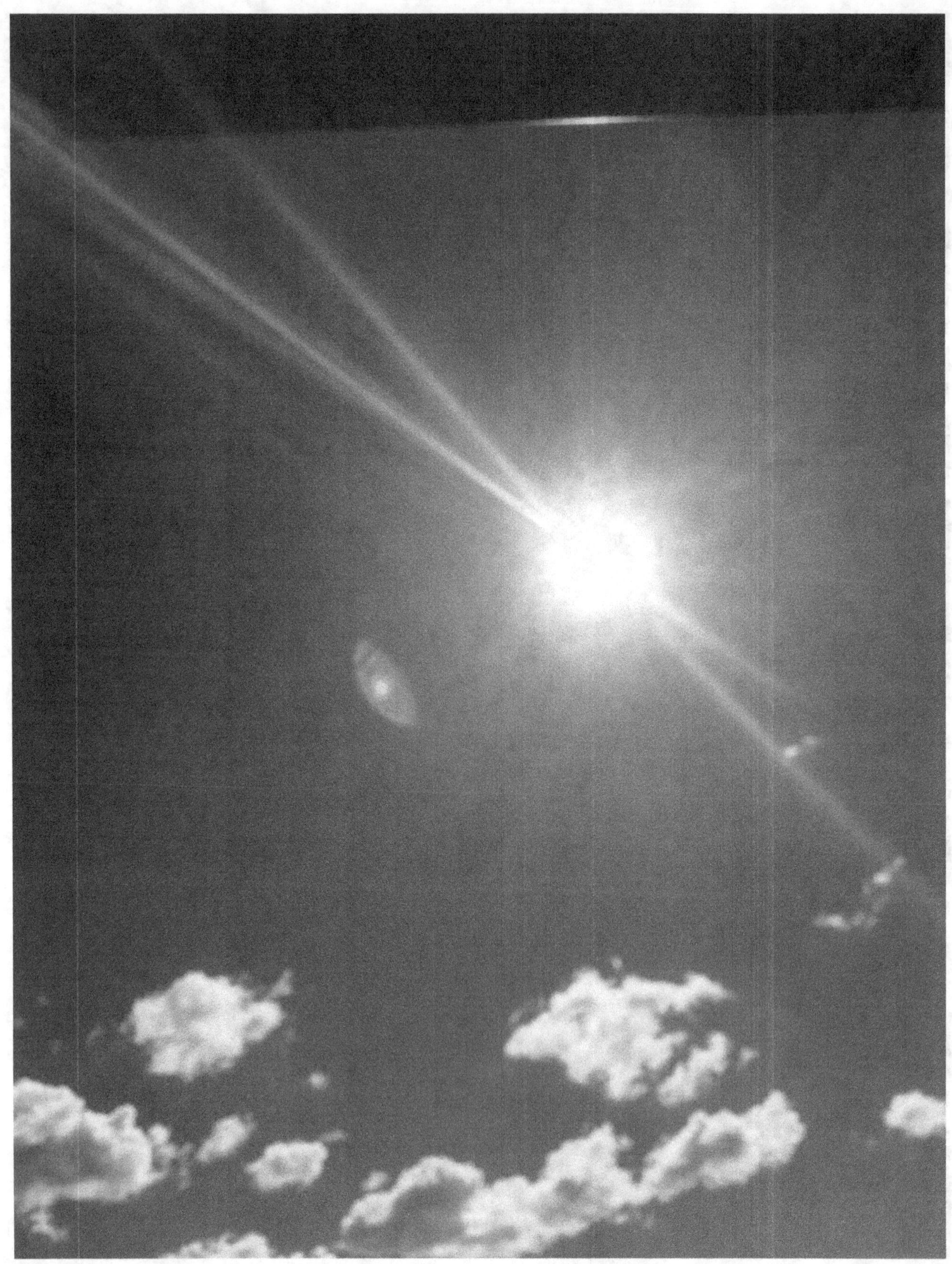

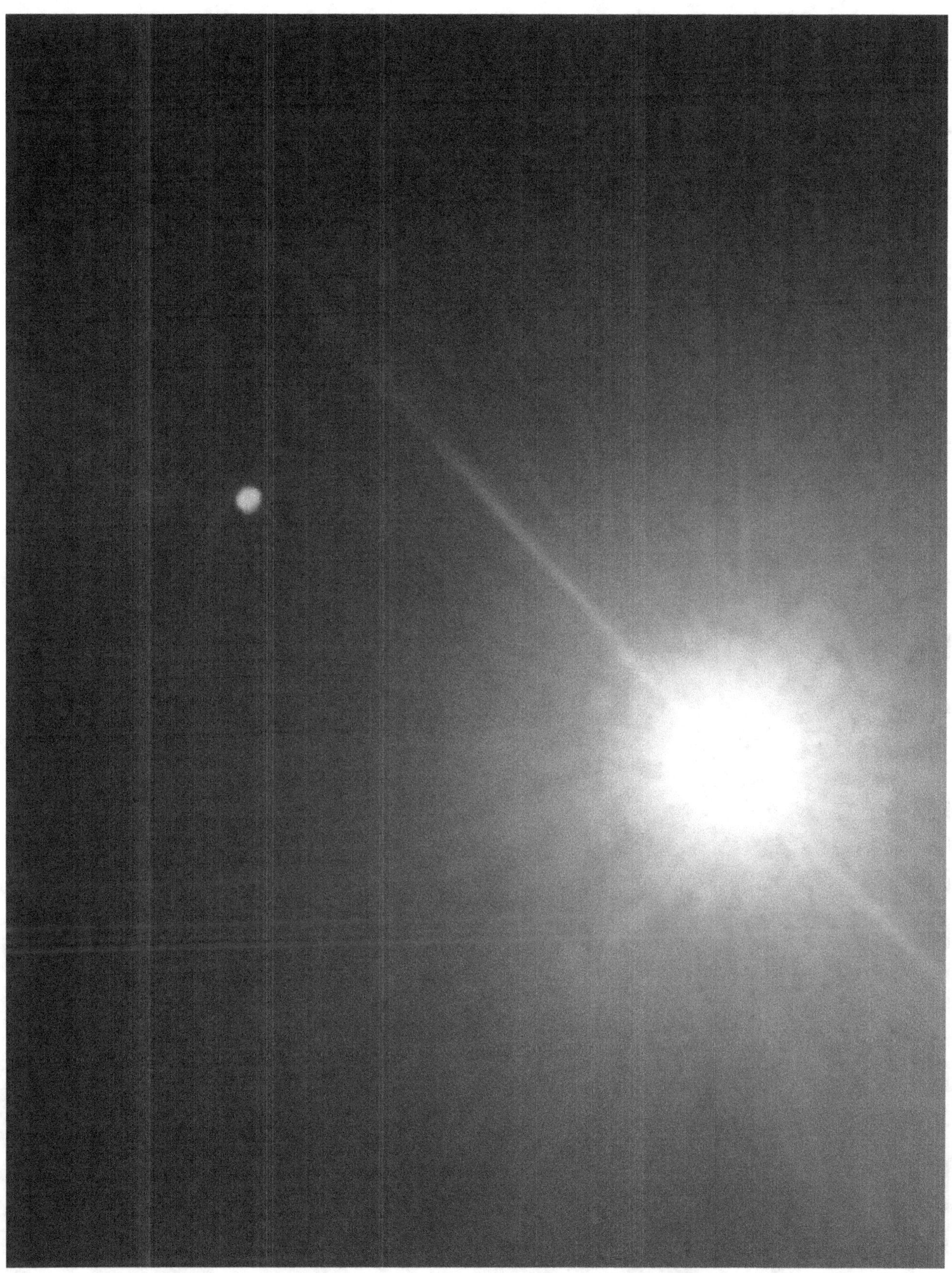

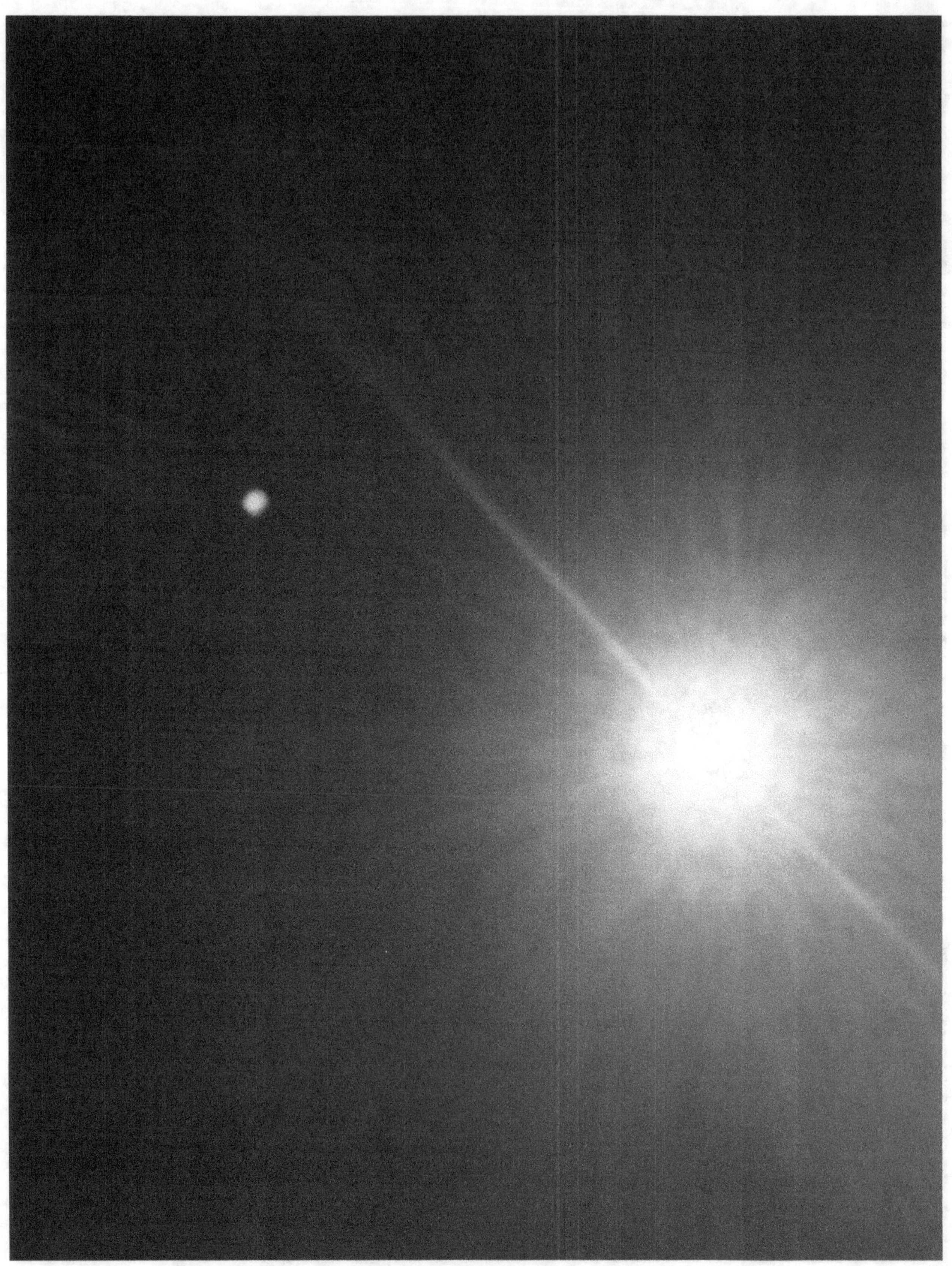

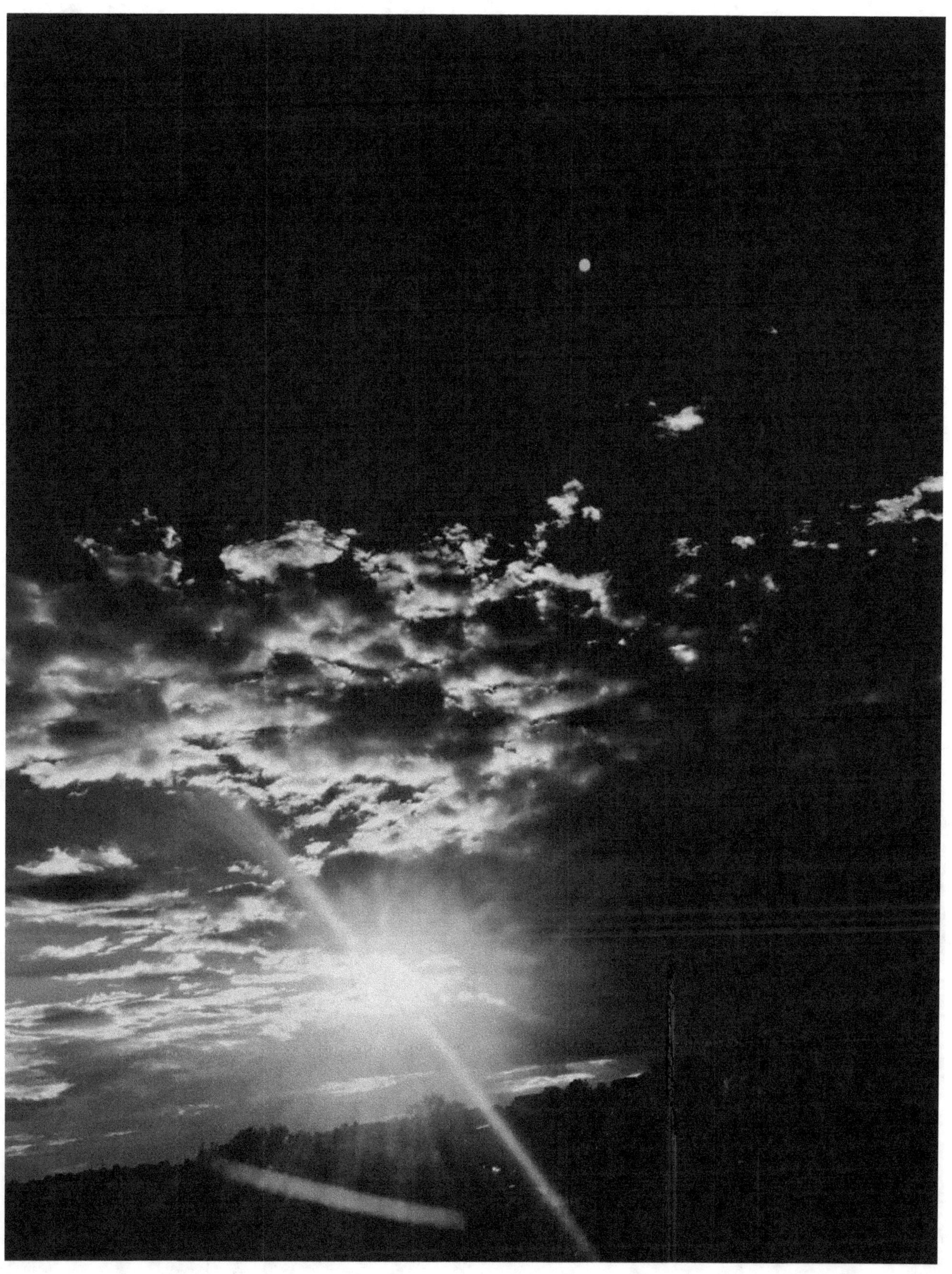

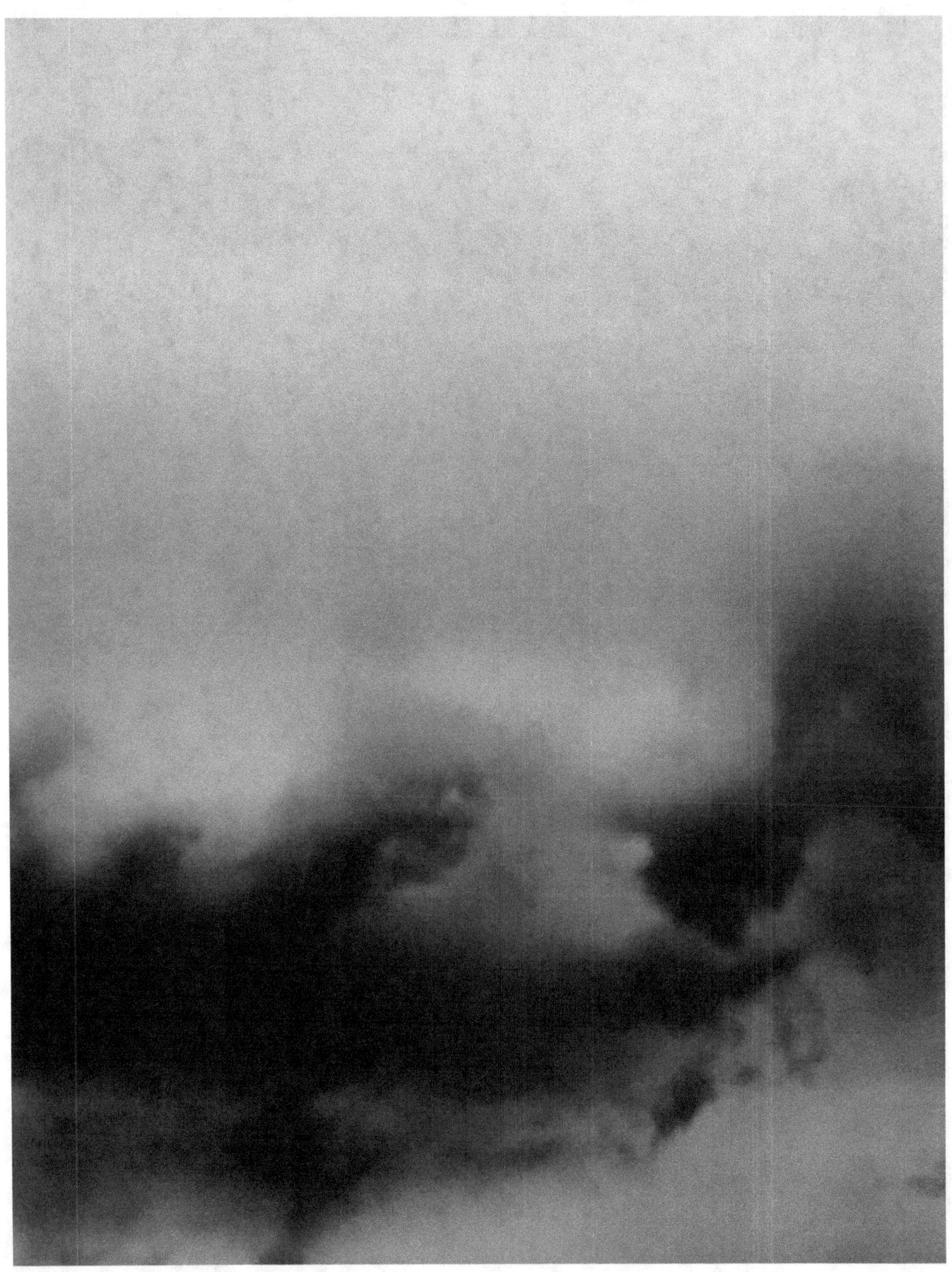

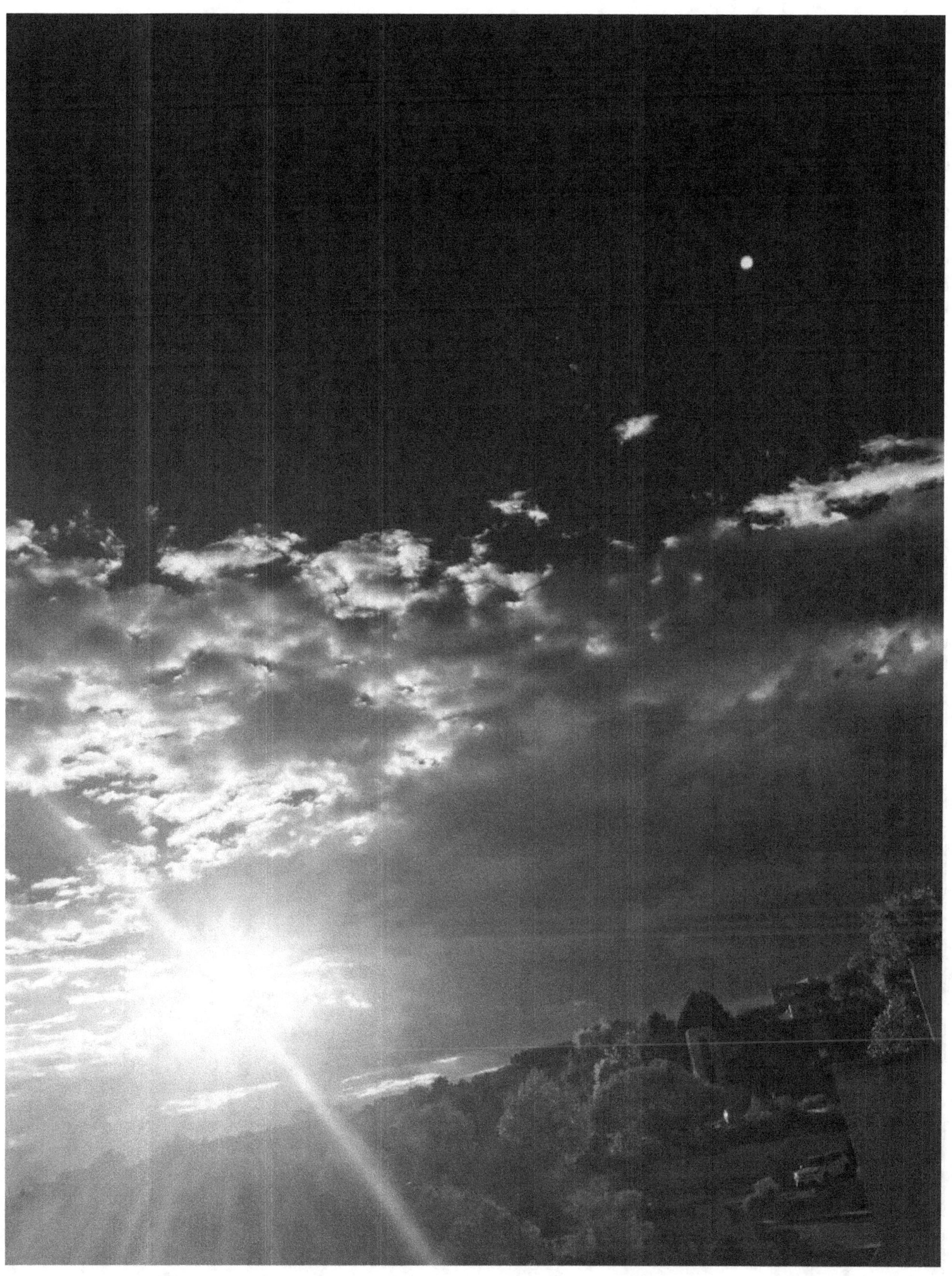

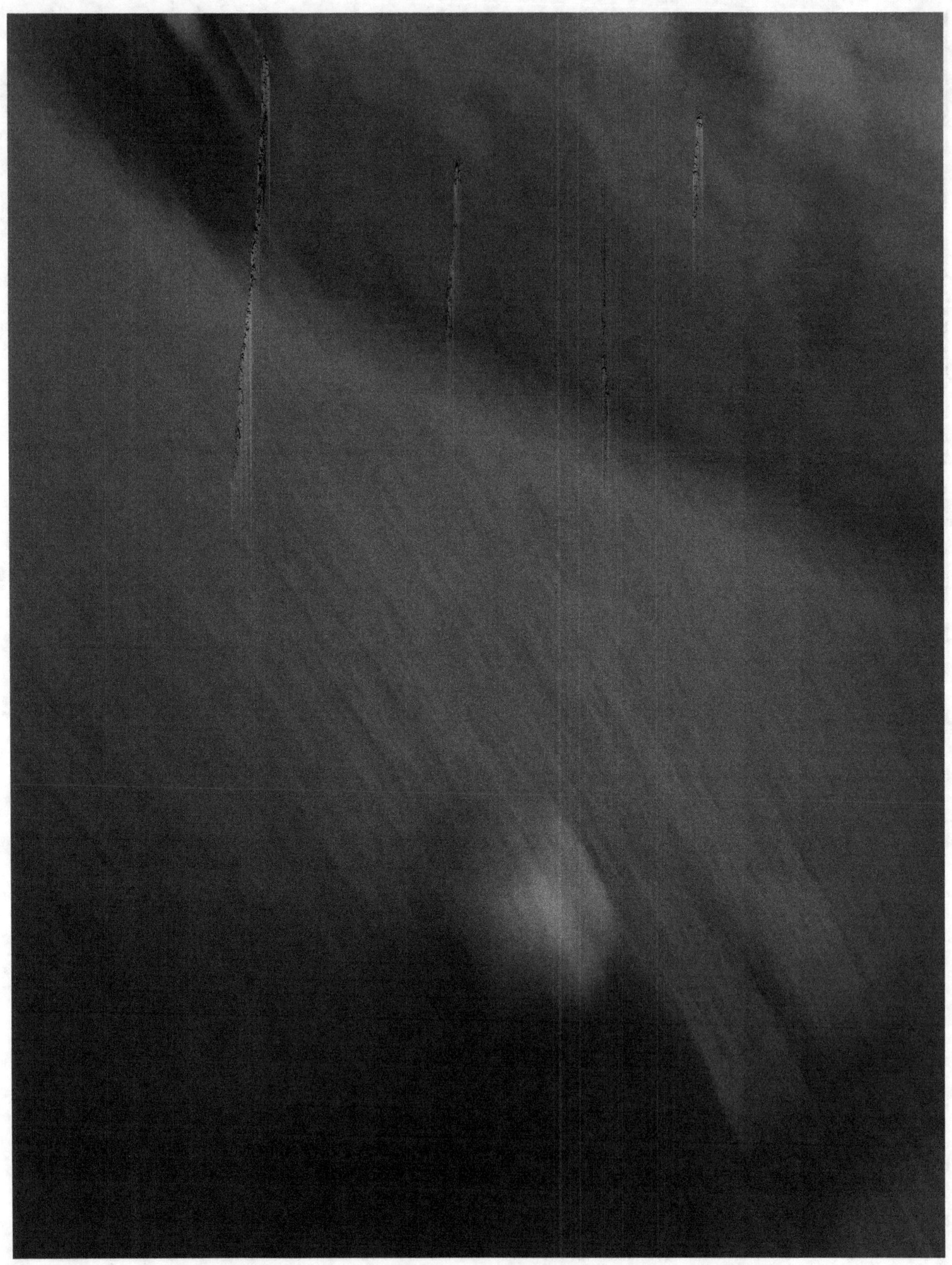